WITNESS
TO
THE
TRUTH

CHRIST
and His Interpreters

BOOKS BY EDITH HAMILTON

WITNESS
TO THE
TRUTH

CHRIST
and His Interpreters

By EDITH HAMILTON

To this end was I born, and for this cause
came I into the world, that I should bear
witness to the truth.
— John 18:37

W · W · NORTON & COMPANY · INC · *New York*

Library of Congress Catalog Card No. 57-7138

PRINTED IN THE UNITED STATES OF AMERICA
FOR THE PUBLISHERS BY THE VAIL-BALLOU PRESS

Contents

Introduction

WHEN THE world we are living in is storm-driven and the bad that happens and the worse that threatens press urgently upon us, there is a strong tendency to emphasize men's baseness or their impotent insignificance. Modern philosophy has turned that way, modern art too. A great change has taken place in the intellectual and artistic atmosphere. Plato's influence through all the centuries up to our own was immensely strong; Platonic philosophy aimed at turning mankind away from baseness, "to lift up the wing of the soul," Plato wrote, "which is renewed and strengthened by the love of the good, the true, the beautiful." Impotence and insignificance were as little stressed as baseness. "All things," he said, "poverty or sickness or any other misfortune will work together for good to him who desires to be like God as far as the nature of man allows." That voice is not heard now in philosophy. Plato's solution was to become like God; the solution of modern philosophy is to die. That is the real fulfillment, we are told, of what Aristotle called "excellence much labored for by the race of men."

So too with art. Pictures, poems, novels, are esteemed in proportion as they show the ugliness and evil and wretchedness of human life. In all the great periods of art the artist looked at the world as its Creator did, and found it good. His aim was to make others share in that vision, to clarify for them the truth of beauty and the beauty of truth. When he had painted his picture or written his poem, people would see truth and beauty where they had not before. His work was with what he thought of as outside himself, and was illuminated by his imagination.

With the arrival of Freud the outer world ceased to be important. Self-knowledge was the clue to truth; in the course of examining oneself and ascribing what one finds there to humanity in general, the idea of what Plato called "Beauty absolute, simple, and everlasting" has become obscured almost to the point of disappearing.

Is this the way the world is to go? That depends upon the people who are living in it. Not only one way is open. We have a choice. Freud was not the first explorer of the inner life. Milleniums ago *Know Thyself* was inscribed at Delphi; and to Socrates self-knowledge was the prelude to any knowledge of the truth. St. Paul was quite as aware of its importance. His idea, however, of the right technique of dealing with it was different from Freud's. "Whatsoever things are true," he wrote, "whatsoever things are just, whatsoever things are pure, whatsoever things are lovely, whatsoever things are of good report, if there be any virtue and if there be any praise, think on these things." To think on them is, as St. Paul knew, to want them to be true, real. We cannot contemplate a world without them; nor need we do so, for whether they shall exist or not is in our hands. Their life depends upon what we do about them. If we do not show them, they will cease to be. "The things that are seen are temporal," St. Paul said, "the things that are not seen are eternal." We have within us the power of seeing the things not seen and of making them visible. The truths that are the most important to us are proved to be true not by reasoning about them or explaining them, but by acting upon them.

It was said of a great English scientist, "He made it easy for people to believe in goodness." Whoever does that in any degree, through an unselfish deed or a courageous word or a compassionate thought, helps others to believe in the indestructibility of goodness; and belief in goodness makes it indestructible. This lifts up the life of every man to an overwhelming importance. All that is good in the world now is in our hands. Upon us depends the reality of God here on the earth today. We alone can give proof that He is. "No man hath seen God at any time. If we love one another God dwelleth in us."

That was the only proof Christ asked from His disciples. He did not ask for belief. The Greek word so translated in the New Testament means primarily trust, and it was this Christ wanted. He did not say to the twelve, "Believe what I am going to tell you about immortality." He said, "You trust God. Trust me too. In my Father's house are many mansions." Belief quickly becomes the conviction of possessing certain knowledge, and that stands in the way of gaining more knowledge. Trust is a deep personal commitment. That is what the picture of Christ's life and death in the Gospels calls forth. "A mighty spiritual force streams forth from Him," says His greatest disciple from his African hospital. "And to those who obey Him He will reveal Himself through all that they are privileged to experience in His fellowship of peace and activity, of struggle and suffering, until they come to know as an inexpressible secret who He is."

There lies the way to the knowledge of the truth. Not by acquiescing in what other people say or have said, not by study and by thought, only by trying to be more compassionate, more understanding, more courageous, by trying to make "the words of my mouth and the meditation of my heart acceptable in thy sight, O Lord, my strength and my redeemer." So and so alone will come deeper and clearer insight into life here and life hereafter. Plato knew. "The soul waiting in wonder and working in reverence for what God shall reveal to her." Christ said, "He that willeth to do the will of God shall know the doctrine, whether it be of God."

The bonds of orthodoxy are loosening; theology becomes less authoritative, but Christ Himself, His life, His spirit, has no less authority. We are conscious as never before of our limitations, of our ignorance, but what He expects of His followers is not more limited; the love that "beareth all things, believeth all things, hopeth all things, endureth all things," that "never faileth," has not become less important. Spiritual heights are here for us to reach as lofty as ever there have been. The consciousness is dawning, the strange and tremendous realization, that upon us depends the living reality of Christ.

God leaves us free. We are free to choose Him or reject Him. No tremendous miracle will come down from heaven to compel us to accept as a fact a Being powerful enough to work it. What would that kind of belief do toward making love or compassion a reality? God puts the truth of Himself into our hands. We must carry the burden of the proof, for His truth can be proved in no other way.

E. H.

I

The Rediscovering of Christ

Never man spake like this man.

—John 7:46

CHRISTIANITY is Christ. "As the branch cannot bear fruit of itself, except it abide in the vine; no more can ye, except ye abide in me." To the degree that he is realized in each generation Christianity lives. To the degree that he seems unreal, remote, wrapped in a mist of strange words and incredible events, Christianity languishes.

Christ must be rediscovered perpetually. It is easy to read beautiful words of his and be moved by them, to accept him vaguely, not scrutinizing closely what has been recorded about him, preferring not to see him sharply in the clear air of truth. It is easy to keep him remote, put away in an atmosphere of unreality where his definite and practical demands to change the basis of human life can be dimmed into a kind of nebulous good will which exacts nothing in particular. But to

11

study the records we have of him, to look at him closely and think out what he really meant, is dismaying because what he demanded Christians do not do and have almost never done. St. Matthew says, "It is enough for the disciple that he be as his master." Christ's disciples have not been as their master. The Christian life as we see it and live it is an easy life. All this and heaven too.

Christianity today makes only private demands. Long ago it ceased making public demands. It has become a home religion. There truthfulness and disinterestedness and what St. Paul called "in honour preferring one another" are held up as standards, but in the world outside no one is expected to follow them. There Christians are indistinguishable from non-Christians. No practical difficulties are presented by a Christian life. This is not Christianity as Christ lived it. What we have turned it into has failed the world.

We must go back to Christ. The record of his life is light shining in the darkness to guide us. We must study it with simplicity, putting aside all that has come between us and it, religious conventions, incomprehensible statements, rituals, magical events. Back of all that mystification Christ stands. He can be found, but it is not easy; he has not only been hidden by the trappings, he has been petrified, sanctified, deified, away from life. We have been taught to read the Gospels in a special way, not going to them to discover the facts about Christ, how he looked to the men who

12

knew him, what he thought about life and death, the way he solved the problems all face. We use the Gospels as a manual of devotion, not a guide-book.

When they are read with serious attention, the kind of study one gives to something to be mastered, the result is startling. It is evident beyond a possibility of doubt that they contradict each other in a way no one could fail to see if he were not under the spell of familiar and venerated words. The evangelists differ when they are relating events as important as Christ's birth, death, resurrection, ascension, differences not trifling or subtle, but as striking as the disagreement about the place where Christ was last seen on earth, which one would suppose would have been ineradicably imprinted on the minds of those who there took leave of him; as important as the record of his last words on the cross, words most of all to be deeply treasured in the hearts of the hearers.

There is no need to multiply examples. They are so many and so plain that anyone who reads the Gospels with attention will perceive them for himself.

Christ is even represented as contradicting himself. Deeds and words are attributed to him which could not have been his except on the assumption that he said one thing at one time and the opposite at another, that he sometimes did what he later condemned. When there are such divergences and disagreements in the only record we have of him it might seem impossible to discover the real Christ, but the truth is that though the evangelists often differ about what he did and what he said, they never differ about what he was. That has been true through the ages. Extraordinarily, the bitter differences that divided Christians, the excommunications, the persecutions, the religious wars, were never due to different opinions about Christ himself. There people have always agreed. Christians fought each other to the death not on what he was, but on how he was to be explained. There are contradictions in the Gospels, but there is nothing contradictory in the person who emerges from them. He is the same, unmistakeable in his individuality, unlike all others there have ever been. What is important is not that the record of him shows inconsistencies, but that he himself is always consistent.

Therefore we can discover him behind what men have done to him, through his own self. It is possible, when the evangelists disagree, to decide which one gives the truth if Christ alone is made the basis of the decision. We can find him if we search for him.

Much is involved in this search. It means looking at the Gospels not only as the saints have seen them, the ladder reaching from man to God, but also as the scholars have considered them, four records which can be traced back from their present form to earlier originals, which were accepted as authoritative only slowly, not until some hun-

14

dred and fifty years after Christ's death, which cannot be understood unless something is known of the influences abroad in the world when they were written.

The Gospels grew. They did not issue complete from the pens of four writers. Matthew, Mark, Luke and John wrote not from firsthand knowledge, but from accounts of Christ they had found written by others, perhaps by men who had known him. And like all writers everywhere those who wrote about him added themselves. It is impossible that only Christ's thoughts and ideas should have been admitted even to the very first records of him. To find what they were, what he himself was, we must seek for him. We must try to dismiss the theories and explanations put forth about him from his day to ours, and we must set aside the current notions abroad when Christianity was taking shape, what everybody believed and what nobody could have conceived that Christ did not believe.

Our task is to keep the picture of him, the living personality, separate from the frame which almost at once was put around it and through the centuries has grown bigger and heavier until often the frame is not seen as a setting for the picture, but the picture there for the sake of the frame.

The difficulty of disengaging Christ from all this is far less than might be expected. The light in the picture is so pure and intense that the ideas and thoughts of others which intrude appear in all their inferiority when that light shines upon them. We can judge the truth and falsehood of all that was said of him and is said of him by himself.

It is remarkable that almost no one outside of the gospel record gives any help toward understanding him. The noble army of saints and martyrs are splendid witnesses to his power over the hearts of men, but they are not marked by their resemblance to him. In that great host St. Paul stands foremost and, astounding proof that he is to the miracle Christ can work within the heart, how different was his temper of mind to that of his master. Even the disciple Christ loved best, who had known him in the intimacy of the daily life of the road, was eager to call down fire from heaven to burn up some inhospitable people, never doubting that Christ would approve. One thinks of the long line of those who, believing they were doing what would most please him, tortured themselves and others and made the test of being his follower the acceptance of a minute point in some bit of finespun theorizing. Which of them all was like him, who never held up suffering as a good, who said of himself that he "came eating and drinking," who declared that men would be judged not by their beliefs, but "Ye shall know them by their fruits," and whose own judgment was, "Neither do I condemn thee: go, and sin no more." That disposition was conspicuous by its absence from the Christian world.

Four hundred years before Christ there lived a man who showed it. He was a Greek, the Athenian Socrates. Of all men anywhere, at any time, he came closest to the pattern Christ held up. His temper of mind was like Christ's. With an extraordinary elevation he combined a soberness and moderation very rare in the lives of the saints. In him as in Christ there was a complete absence of ecstasies and transports. Even St. Paul, who was not given to them, knew a man, "whether in the body or out of the body" he could not say, who was "caught up to the third heaven," and as so often he pointed the way the church was to take. It was as little Socrates' way as it was Christ's. The object each held before him was one which signally could not be reached through raptures and fervours of feeling; truth, the Spirit of truth, Christ said to his disciples, would guide them into all truth. Socrates' aim too was to arouse men to find that guidance. He knew as Christ did that truth can never be found for men, but only by men. Christ said, "Seek and ye shall find." Find what? That he did not say. The conditions of finding he put into clear words. He that wills to do the will of God shall know. The only way to find the truth is to live it. The pure in heart shall see God. He said, "I am the truth." He was what he taught.

So in his degree was Socrates. He showed in himself what he urged men to seek. He put before them a new life: they were to be servants of the

17

truth and so of God. Looking at him they understood what that meant. He realized it for them; he
was the ideal he held up to them.

Even of old the Christian world, so bitterly
antagonistic to any ideas not specifically contained
in their creeds and dogmas, made an exception
in Socrates' case. They recognized his likeness to
Christ. He was the example that a soul could be
Christlike not through grace, but by nature.
Erasmus said, "Holy Socrates, pray for us."

To know him is a help to knowing Christ, and
it is not hard to know him. We can see him quite
clearly. Plato who drew his portrait, could not,
of course, keep himself out of it, any more than
Christ's recorders could, but at least magic did
not dog Plato's footsteps as it did everyone's
footsteps when the Gospels were written. In the
fourth century B.C. Greeks had no leaning to
marvels. Also in the centuries that followed no one
founded a church on Socrates and built up around
him a theology and hung creeds and ceremonials
upon him. To see what he was we do not have to
brush anything away except a bit of Plato. We can
use him as a stepping stone to Christ, a first aid in
realizing what Christ was.

He was Christ's forerunner. Christ's foremost
follower was St. Paul. He is always called the
founder of the Christian church, he not Christ,
because Christ had no thought of starting a new
religion, and the idea of connecting him with an

organization appears instantly as a manifest absurdity. But the thought and the idea were both strongly present in Paul. He said very little about truth, a great deal about particular truths which to him separated Christians from all others. He was the first Christian theologian. Here too he started the church on its way. Christ had never explained himself and had never explained God. Paul explained them both. The endless bitter, and often bloody, disputes which have tried for nineteen hundred years to settle questions to which Christ never gave a moment's attention, go back to him.

But this was only a part of him and a small part. He was in his day, and he remains to this day, the most shining example of what Christ can do, of the miracles Christ works. He was changed from a fanatic on fire with fanaticism's cruelty and arrogance into one who lived and died for the love of Christ and expressed as no one else ever did the spirit of love. He expressed too, as no one outside of the Old Testament has done, the evil that men confront within themselves, "the sin which doth so easily beset us." He knew it to the depths from his past and how it could be overcome. In all the great cloud of witnesses for Christ which surrounds us as we run the race set before us, he is the chief.

We must go back to Christ or we shall lose Christianity. In the quest for him Socrates and

St. Paul are guides; the one to an understanding of the man who walked the roads of Galilee and lived and died for the truth; the other to the power of Christ through whom Paul found the complete and final victory over himself.

II

Socrates

And ye shall know the truth
and the truth shall set you free.
—John 8:32

FOR THIS CAUSE came I into the world, that I should bear witness unto the truth." The words are in the Gospel of John, spoken by Christ to Pilate. Christ's witness to the truth was himself. He had no system of thought which could be considered apart from himself. It is clear that he took no care to pass on to future generations accurate statements of what he knew. He never wrote anything down. He seemed intent only on reaching the men he met day by day, and he said little to them by way of explanation. He left behind him what one man and another remembered of his sayings; in the Gospel of John he is quoted as saying that the Holy Spirit would bring to the remembrance of his disciples all that he had said to them, but he himself left only the record of his own life. It would seem beyond doubt that he believed the truth he knew could be expressed in no other way.

Socrates too never tried to put the truth he had found into words. He thought as Christ did that it was impossible to tell men what it was and then expect them to know it. He too had no ordered philosophy or theology and he too never wrote a word down. Like Christ he lived his truth and died for it. A life can be more lasting than systems of thought. Socrates has outlasted two millenniums.

He was a witness to all that is contained in the word goodness, to its reality and its power. It was said of a great English scientist, "He made it easy for people to believe in goodness." This Socrates did as few since the beginning of history. No one who knew him could doubt that, as he said, "Goodness has a most real and actual existence." He left the memory of a life which conquered through it, which was never defeated though he was imprisoned and put to death, and which has been kept in men's memories among the things that are eternal. During the four hundred years between his death and Christ's the Greek and the Roman world turned to him to learn how to live, and ever since men have seen through him the changelessness of the truth, the enduring verity of what he lived by. "That which existing among men is the form and likeness of God," Plato said.

He lived during the great age of Greece, in Athens of the fifth century B. C. No figure was more familiar there than his. He did not teach from some pulpit or teacher's desk, withdrawn from men in order to think great thoughts or to find God. The busy life of the city was his life. He knew everybody and everybody knew him. Wherever men met he was at home. In a sense he did not teach at all. He just talked spontaneously on anything that happened to come up as he walked the streets or went into a gymnasium or dined with a friend. He never thought, or at any rate he never spoke, about mankind or humanity or society or the public. What he was interested in was each individual he met. He felt an intense, overwhelming, desire for the good of that particular person. Nothing could have been farther from him than the idea that for hundreds of years after his death people would turn to him for light. He never gave a thought to the future. He wanted good things for the Athenians whom he saw every day and whom he knew and loved and understood, and he wanted, so greatly, to open, at least a little bit, the eyes of that delightful young fellow who had just come up to him, or speak a word to that anxious father who was troubled about his son.

Athens was more and more hard pressed during his later life; she was at war and hardships were the order of the day but there was always time to stop and hear what Socrates was saying. He had a genius for conversation and the keen-witted Athenians were an eager audience. They were fighting, but they were thinking too, and ideas were very important. One of Plato's dialogues in which Socrates is the speaker begins: "Yesterday evening I got back from the army and I went straight to the gymnasium near the Archon's porch and found a number of people I knew. I was quite unexpected and they all greeted me and asked, 'However did you escape?' 'Well,' I replied, 'you see I am here.' 'It's reported that the battle went badly and many people we knew fell.' 'Not far from the truth,' I said. 'You were there?' 'Yes.' 'Well then, do sit down and tell us all about it.' So I sat down and gave them the news from the army. But when there had been enough of this I began to ask them how things were going on at home, especially how the pursuit of philosophy was prospering."

That is what Athens was like during the greater part of Socrates' life. The importance of "philosophy," the search for wisdom, for the truth, never lapsed or receded into the background, and he was happy and at home there. But later a change came over the city. The war with Sparta lasted twenty-seven years and ended in total defeat for the Athenians. It shook the moral and spiritual foundations of Athens and brought a great part of them crashing down. The old ideas of right and wrong seemed shown up as false or at the least futile. The Spartan idea of what was good and desirable was quite unlike the Athenian, and the Spartans won the war. By every realistic standard they proved that what they thought was right and what the Athenians thought was wrong. The great historian of the war, Thucydides, says the whole point of view in Athens changed, the very meaning of words was altered, vices were praised, virtues despised. The reckless disregard of life was held to be fine and courageous; kindness and generosity were scorned as proofs of softness and weakness.

The lowest depth was reached when the city put Socrates to death. That was in 399, five years after the war ended, when he was seventy years old. The charge was "Impiety," that he had induced the young men of the city to give up believing in the state religion which was still Homer's jovial, amoral Olympians, impossible for any thinking person to take seriously. The indictment ran: "Socrates is an evil-doer and a corrupter of young men because he does not receive the gods the state receives, but introduces new divinities." It would seem natural enough in any Christian country up to a comparatively short time ago for a man to be executed and tortured, too, for doing that, but it was not natural in Greece. In all the history of Athens we know of only four persons who were persecuted for their opinions and of the four, Socrates alone suffered the death penalty. But by that time Athens was ruined, overwhelmed by all that a crushing defeat brings to a proud people. The Athenians had lost their faith in everything they had stood for, their courage, too. They were a crushed, humiliated people, and they were afraid. They could not face the future; they could only look back, with an agony of regret for what they had lost. The passion for freedom, the instinct for reasonableness, which had marked them beyond all other qualities, were swept away in a wave of reaction. Socrates had new ideas; the gods he believed in had not the slightest resemblance to the old, and only the old was dear at that moment of Athens' misery. The city which had been given to hospitality to men of all sorts and conditions of opinions, and which hundreds of years later, St. Paul reported, was desirous of nothing so much as to hear something new, condemned to death her best and greatest citizen because he taught a new religion. And for a moment Athens was satisfied that she had taken a step back to the familiar and the safe and away from the dark menace of the future.

As a teacher of religion Socrates was a very odd figure, an evangelist such as there has never been before or since. He lived in an evil day, but he never denounced any of the evils. He never thundered anathemas as the men of righteousness have had the habit of doing against the wickedness of their times. Nothing could appear less like Isaiah and Jeremiah and all the other passionate reformers through the ages than he does as we see him in Plato's pages, so gentle, urbane, and companionable, thinking only of winning men over, persuading them, convincing them, never denouncing or threatening them.

His temper of mind was all the other way. He

did not look at people with stern disapproval; he liked them. Their ways did not irritate or anger him; they did often amuse him. He had a gay spirit; he saw the world with a humourous eye. "Bless me," he said, looking around in the market where all an Athenian wanted lay piled in glowing profusion, "what a lot of things there are a man can do without." In the brilliant society of Periclean Athens he was welcomed everywhere as the best of company. He had but to enter a gymnasium, that Athenian equivalent of a club, and eager young men gathered around him, greeting him as a boon companion, joking with him and making fun of him, with an undertone of loving delight in him. They really caught a glimpse of something lofty and beautiful in him never seen before.

He had a wonderful gift for making people feel at home with him. He did not seem to be trying to instruct them; he put forward no claim to know better than they did. He had a most disarming way of talking, a great taste for homely illustration and a great distaste for high-sounding talk, out of which, however, he got much amusement when anybody indulged in it. No one could be less pretentious. He seemed always to imply, "I know I may be quite wrong." And this was not merely his manner; he really had no fixed creed, no set of doctrines, which he felt he must make others believe. He had a profound conviction which ruled his life and which it was the effort of his life to communicate, but it did not present itself to him as a series of truths which it was imperative for all to accept. As a Greek his mind did not work that way. Greek religion was developed not by priests or prophets or saints, but by poets and artists and philosophers, all of them people who instinctively leave thought free. The Greeks had no sacred book, no creed, no ten commandments, no church. The very idea of orthodoxy was unknown to them. They would have resented or laughed at anyone who told them they must believe thus and so. An Athenian's dearest right was to think for himself and he used it to the full.

So Socrates was only going along with his hearers when he declined to do their thinking for them. What he wanted was something much more difficult than that. Aristotle says happiness is activity of soul. It is a precise description of Socrates' way of making men happy. "God has sent me to attack this city," he told the Athenians, "as if it were a great horse sluggish from its size, which needs to be aroused by a gadfly. I think I am that gadfly. I will never cease from exhorting you: Are you not ashamed of caring so much for money and for reputation and for honour? Will you not think about wisdom and truth and what is good for your souls?" He would sting them into activity to see for themselves; he would not show them what they ought to see. His talks with them usually ended in some such fashion, as, "This may be true, but is also quite likely to be untrue,

30

and therefore I would not have you too easily persuaded. Reflect well—and when you have found the truth, come and tell me."

No one less dogmatic ever lived. He spent his life in the search for the truth; it was all-important to him, but he did not leave behind him one hard and fast definition. He never stated, he only suggested—with a question mark. In his speech at his trial he spoke of "a divine agency which comes to me, a sign, a kind of a voice, which I was first conscious of as a child. It never commands me to do anything, but it does forbid me." That was all. He made no attempt to clarify or classify the experience; he knew he could not imprison within a formula the truth he saw. "To find the Maker and Father of all is hard," he said, "and having found him it is impossible to utter him."

But underneath this inconclusiveness was a clear purpose and a definite method. "The unexamined life is not worth living," he said. Each man must examine his own, look at himself, at what he is, in the light of the truth he could find if he sought for it. Socrates never offered to lead him to it. As he saw it, that would mean little. Only what each man discovered for himself could be actually true to him. The truth he accepted at secondhand on the word of another remained always unreal to him. The one way to help men was to make them want to find. "Although my mind is far from wise," he said, "some of those who come to me make astonishing progress. They

31

discover for themselves, not from me—and yet
I am an instrument in the hands of God."

He was always the seeker, inquiring, not in-
structing, but his questions upset men's confidence in themselves and the comfortable conventions they lived by. "Laches, you are a soldier. Tell
me, if you can, what is courage." "Indeed, Socrates, that is not difficult. He is courageous who does
not run from the enemy, but stays at his post and
fights." "Very good, Laches, but I see I did not
express myself clearly. May not another man who
fights by running from the enemy also be courageous?" "Why, Socrates, I do not understand."
"Well, Laches, the Scythians fight by flying as
well as by pursuing." "You are right, Socrates, but
they are cavalry, not the heavy-armed Greek I
was speaking of." "Yes, Laches, and I see I put
my question badly. I meant to ask not only about
the courage of heavy-armed soldiers, but of cavalry
too, and not only those courageous in war, but in
perils by sea and in disease and in poverty, and
also those who have courage against their own
desires as well as against fear and pain. What is
that quality common to all these cases which we
call courage?"

The first effect he had upon his hearers was
usually perplexity and bewilderment, sometimes
it was extreme distress. Alcibiades, most brilliant
in that brilliant town, told the company at the din-
ner table in the Symposium, "I have heard Pericles
and other great orators, but they never troubled

me or made me angry at living a life no more worth living than a slave's life. But this man has often brought me to such a pass that I could hardly endure to go on as I was, neglecting what my soul needs. I have sometimes wished that he was dead."

That is how he could shake men's dispositions, although he himself would have said, It is not I. It is that they have found within themselves the light and in that clear shining they see the darkness they are living in and the meanness of their souls.

What he really was doing as he talked so easily and familiarly and humourously to the men of Athens, as he lived day by day so courteously and modestly and unobtrusively in his city that he loved, was establishing a new standard for the world. He believed with an unshakeable conviction that goodness and truth were the fundamental realities and that every human being had the capacity to attain to them. All men had within them a guide, a spark of the true light which could lead them to the full light of truth. This was Socrates' basic belief, in the words of the Gospel of John, "The true Light which lighteth every man that cometh into the world." His own mission he believed was to open blind eyes, to make men realize the darkness of their ignorance and evil and so to arouse in them a longing for the light; to induce them to seek until they caught a glimpse of the eternal truth and goodness "without variableness or shadow of turning" which underlay life's confusions and futilities. If once they could be shown them, could behold them in their beauty, they would inevitably, irresistibly, seek for a fuller and fuller sight. When men have attained to a perception of what Aristotle called "Excellence, much laboured for by the race of mortals," they do not let the vision go. Great thoughts endure. The false and the trivial pass away. And what is true of the race of men is true of the individual. Men are not able, it is not in them as human beings, if once they see the shining of the truth, to blot it out completely and forget it. We needs must love the highest when we see it. That is the great Socratic dogma.

Outside, in the wretched war-wracked city, all was in confusion, but everyone could create order in the one part of the world which was actually his own, his soul. The laws and the authority of the state might break down, but the laws of the life within, self-mastery, self-control, could not be touched by anything outside. And he who realized the divine order in himself made the great contribution toward bringing it into existence in the world. As St. Paul was to say four hundred years later, "The law of God after the inward man."

This was a new religion. Its centre was the soul. In that world of shaken moral values where people were saying, "Life is too short to find out if there are gods or not. Let us eat and drink, for tomorrow we die," Socrates came declaring that morality had an unshakeable foundation. The good, "that

34

through whose presence the good are good," could be found by all. Morality was "of the nature of things"—human nature. "A good man in his dark strivings is somehow conscious of the right way." Goethe was truly Socratic when he said that. Each soul, Socrates believed, had the seed of divinity, the potentiality of finding the underlying reality, which in another aspect is God, and of realizing the moral order. Therefore, each was of supreme importance. "The things of men," he said, were what a man should be concerned about. Cicero understood him when he wrote, "He brought philosophy down from heaven into the cities and homes of men." He himself would altogether have agreed. Yes, he would have said, because those are the places of importance, the places where men dwell. Philosophy, which is the love of the truth, must come down and live with mankind, the only seekers and discoverers of it. Men have the highest destiny. They can know the truth.

It was the one concern of his life that they should find it. They were so made that only then, only when they had beheld the truth and their souls were penetrated by its goodness and its beauty, could they really live, fulfilling at last their own nature, in harmony with reality, with God. Centuries later St. Augustine said: "Thou hast made us for thyself and restless are our hearts until they rest in thee."

But it is not only or even chiefly through his

faith in man and in God that he has lived for nearly two thousand five hundred years. It is because of what he himself was. He proved the truth of what he said by his life and even more by his death. He showed men what they could become, their own spiritual possibilities, and he showed them how they could meet "the mighty stranger, death." This great lesson was not obscured by later legends of marvels and miracles. No magical doings were ever related of Socrates.

Strongest of all was the overpowering impression made by the last days of his life. Throughout them he had as throughout his life a heart at leisure from itself. When he was arrested and taken to court he met his accusers in a spirit of kindly good will. He refused to save his life by promising to give up teaching, but he did so with complete courtesy. He told them that would mean leaving the post where God had placed him and "Strange indeed would my conduct be, O men of Athens, if I who (on the battlefield) remained where the generals placed me, facing death like any other man, if now when God orders me, I were to desert through fear of death. Men of Athens, I honour you and love you, but I shall obey God rather than you. And to you and to God I commit my cause, to be determined by you as is best for you and for me."

When the sentence of death had been pronounced he ended his reply to it by comforting his judges for condemning him. "Be of good

cheer," he told them, "and know of a certainty
that no evil can happen to a good man either in
life or after death. I see clearly that the time has
come when it is better for me to die, and so my
accusers have done me no harm. Still—they did
not mean to do me good, and for this I may gently
blame them. And now we go our ways, you to live
and I to die. Which is better, only God knows."

In his prison cell he was serene, sometimes
humourous, always perfectly natural, just himself,
sweetly thoughtful of the men who loved him and
of what they were suffering for him, but showing
no suffering on his own behalf. He was ready to
meet death peacefully, entirely fearless. One who
was there with him said to another who had been
away from the city at the time: "I could not pity
him. He seemed to me beyond that. I thought of
him as blessed. I thought that he would be happy
in the other world. What I felt was a strange mix-
ture of pleasure and pain."

In prison a devoted friend, Crito, came to him,
begging him, "O my beloved Socrates, let me
entreat you to escape. Let us who can well afford
it, bribe your way out of prison. Oh, be persuaded." Socrates answered serenely, "No. That
cannot be. No one may do wrong intentionally.
I will not break the law to save my life. I shall die,
but I shall die innocent of wrong. This, dear Crito,
is what a voice I seem to hear says to me and it
prevents me from hearing any other. Yet speak, if
you have something to say." "Socrates, I have

nothing to say." "Then leave me, Crito, to fulfill the will of God and to follow whither he leads."

When the time came for him to drink the hemlock he had a kind word for the jailer who brought him the cup, and "quite readily and cheerfully," the narrator tells us, "he drank off the poison. In spite of my efforts my tears flowed fast. I wept, not for him, but for myself. So all of us were cowards except Socrates. He remained serene."

The talk that day in the prison had been of the immortal life and Socrates had told his friends, "Our venture is a glorious one. The soul with her own proper jewels which are justice and courage and nobility and truth, in these arrayed she is ready to go on her journey when her time comes." He broke off his discourse by exclaiming, "But I really must go and bathe so that the women may not have the trouble of washing my body when I am dead." Crito suddenly recalled from the delight of hearing him talk, to the stark facts, cried out, "How shall we bury you?" "In any way you like," was the amused answer. "Only be sure that you get hold of me and see that I do not run away." And turning to the others of the gathering, "I cannot make this fellow realize that the dead body will not be me. Don't let him talk about burying Socrates, for false words infect the soul. Dear Crito, say only that you are burying my body."

Some fifty years after his death Aristotle, who knew him well through Plato, surely had him in mind when he wrote: "There is a life which is higher than the measure of humanity. Men live it not by virtue of their humanity, but by virtue of something in them that is divine." Looking at Socrates, the Greek and Roman world knew that that had been done. A human life had been lived divinely and they took courage for their own lives.

His intensity of conviction is what we are left with. Men can know what is true. And yet just before he died, in his last talk with his friends, for a moment he faltered. He was face to face with death. He was looking into the darkness not when he was enfeebled by illness, not grown weak so that thought was impossible and the eyes of the mind were closing along with those of the body to forget and drift away in sleep. His powers were strong, his intellect vigourously alive. What was he to meet after he drank the poison? Immortality or extinction? He had maintained earlier in the day to those gathered around him, that he "had reason to be of good cheer when he was about to die, and that after death he might hope to obtain the greatest good in the other world," but as the argument went on, as he tried with all his powers to think through whether the soul was in actual, factual, truth immortal, he felt within himself a doubt. All that he had striven for, to see the clear light of the truth, to arouse in others the longing to see it, to lift men up to find the reality of the good, the reality of God, upon which all that there is depends—was this to end in blank nothingness? That was what he faced and the darkness rolled over him as it did when Christ faced it upon the cross. But through the final anguish of doubt the anchor of his whole life, the pure devotion to the truth, held fast. His words are: "At this moment I know that I have not the temper of a seeker after the truth. I am only a partisan—who always cares nothing about the rights of a question, but only to convince his hearers. The sole difference between such a one and me at this moment is that he wants to convince his hearers and I want to convince myself. Think how much I have to gain if I can do this. If the soul is immortal, then it is well for me to believe it. If there is nothing after death, then during the short time still left me my wrong belief cannot lead me into any harm. This is my state of mind as I begin the discussion. And I would ask you to be thinking of the truth and not of Socrates. Agree with me if I seem to you to be speaking the truth; if not, oppose me with might and main that I may not in my desire deceive you as well as myself, and like the bee, leave my sting in you before I die. —And now let us proceed."

So Socrates loved the truth and so he made it live. He brought it down into the homes and hearts of men because he showed it to them in himself, the spirit of truth manifest in the only way that can be, in the flesh.

III

How the Gospels Were Written

And the Pharisees . . . began to question with him, seeking of him a sign from heaven. . . . And he sighed deeply in his spirit, and saith, Why doth this generation seek after a sign? Verily I say unto you, There shall no sign be given. . . .

—Mark 8:11, 12

SOCRATES' TEACHING stands out as singularly consistent. Plato, his chief reporter, had one of the greatest minds there has ever been, and contradictions could hardly have crept into his account without his perceiving it. But in the long history of religious thought the very opposite is oftenest seen. To be sure, men have shown the ability in all ages and on most subjects to entertain ideas which contradict each other, but because of religion's insistent claim, the examples furnished by religious men are especially conspicuous. Some of the greatest Christian scholars and saints have contributed to them. Accepting Christ's words as the truth itself, they have again and again asserted what went against his plainest teaching. St. Augustine is said to have loved to repeat, "Suffer little children to come unto me, and forbid them not." Yet he was the fervent advocate, even very probably the author, of the dogma that unbaptized children are banished forever from heaven. Thomas à Kempis set himself to teach men how to imitate Christ, yet he could urge them to do the very reverse. "It is praiseworthy," he writes, "for a religious man to have no wish to see men. If thou wouldst have true peace, thou must keep thine eyes upon thyself alone." He had read the Gospels with loving devotion, nevertheless he said what could be true for a follower of Christ only if the forty days in the desert were all that was known of his life.

Directly contradictory statements can be accepted with a wonderful ease when they are endeared by long usage in a religious book. One of the best known and most loved of the psalms declares: "For thou desirest not sacrifice; else would I give it: thou delightest not in burnt offering. The sacrifices of God are a broken spirit: a broken and a contrite heart, O God, thou wilt not despise." With a brief intervening verse about rebuilding Jerusalem, the psalm continues: "Then shalt thou be pleased with the sacrifices of righteousness, with burnt offering and whole burnt offering: then shall they offer bullocks upon thine altar." Quite possibly this last verse is a later addition; even so, the fact remains that the author of it did not see that the two assertions were incompatible, any more than the numberless people who have loved and accepted both as the word of God for several millenniums.

44

But the great example of the power to ignore contradictions was the belief in the verbal inspiration of the Bible. No doubt the motive was strong. It freed men from all personal responsibility. The idea that every word in the Hebrew—or Greek—or Latin—or English—Bible was a direct revelation from God lifted the burden and was infinitely comfortable. Yet even so, it is no less than wonderful that one single thoughtful person could have held to it, let alone the whole Christian church for hundreds of years. But the many and plain contradictions were ignored. What men demanded and would have was the revelation of absolute truth independent of human effort, a book inscribed by the hand of God. The idea of an infallible Bible was irresistible when once it had been conceived.

And yet it was a comparatively late idea. For hundreds of years the Old Testament was altered and added to, and writings that have now no place in it were esteemed equally with the others. Just when the great Hebrew teachers finally decided what was and what was not the word of God is not known, but it was some time after the birth of Christ. Of course with this decision the book grew progressively more holy until every letter was divine and any alteration blasphemous.

The New Testament went through much the same process. The new is never holy. A certain length of time had to pass before Christian writings could in the eyes of the Christian Jews reach the same status as the Old Testament. The first statement we know of that the Gospels were sacrosanct and immutable must be dated some hundred and fifty years after the death of Christ, and they were almost certainly the first in the New Testament to reach that height.

The century and a half when the Gospels were taking shape and advancing in men's esteem until they were held in equal honour with the Old Testament as the Word of God, is the period when we know less about Christianity than at any other time in its history, with the exception of the first thirty years or so which are covered by the Acts of the Apostles, the earliest account we have.

This is a real history of the Christian church directly after Christ's death. It ends with St. Paul a prisoner in Rome. We are not told anything further, not even how he died. The writer does not bring his book to an end, he simply stops writing. Two major calamities overtook the Christians around that time, Nero's persecution in the year 64 which brought terrible suffering to the church in Rome—St. Paul is supposed to have been killed then—and soon after, acute disturbances in Jerusalem which culminated in the capture of the city by the Romans and the destruction of the temple, a catastrophe hardly more shattering to the Jews than to the Christians. It is open to wonder why even in these circumstances of terror and anguish Paul's death was left unrecorded, but it is perfectly clear why the history of

the Christian church was not continued. With
the destruction of Jerusalem there was no Christian church as Acts had pictured it. That church
had been in Jerusalem, an authority for all Christians. It was in Jerusalem that the apostles lived;
from Jerusalem that directions were sent to the
Christian communities in other cities what to do
and what to believe; to Jerusalem that St. Paul
turned when the orthodoxy of his teaching was
called into question. When Jerusalem fell, the
church in that sense came to an end; there was
no longer one authoritative center for Christians.

They must in large part have fled from the deso-
lated city. In a few years they must have been scattered widely through Palestine, Asia Minor and
still farther afield. Tradition, more to be depended
on than is generally believed, sends St. Peter to
Rome and St. John to Ephesus, places distant from
each other by weeks of traveling. There was no
unifying force at work anywhere. The mother
church had ceased to be; the great organizing mis-
sionary Paul was dead. All that was left were the
churches he and his companions had founded,
little gatherings in this place and that where a few
people would come together to pray, each tiny
church after the fall of Jerusalem forced to depend
upon itself. They had their own Christian experience to guide them; they had stories about Christ
told by his disciples; perhaps they had one of St.
Paul's Epistles, but there is reason to believe that
they had nothing else, that there was as yet no

written record of Christ's life. That is certainly what St. Paul's attitude implies and St. Luke's in the Acts, but it is a very surprising implication. Could it be possible that no life of Christ was written for a whole generation after his death? Surely one would expect that those who had lived with him and loved him would have begun as soon as he left them to preserve in writing their precious memories of him while they were still vivid. But St. Paul, the earliest Christian writer we know of, shows a marked indifference to the subject, and St. Luke, the earliest Christian historian, shows exactly the same. St. Paul rarely speaks of anything Christ did, and quotes him almost never. He really seems to have thought that to dwell upon what Christ was on earth would not be advisable for a Christian. He says, "Though we have known Christ after the flesh, yet henceforth know we him no more." These words seem a little less strange, perhaps, when one reflects that Paul never did know Christ "after the flesh," while he was on earth. The Christ of his vision was all in all to him. But the explanation, hardly satisfactory even in his case, fails entirely in the case of Christ's own disciples, all of whom St. Luke represents in the Acts as feeling in precisely the same way. They are living in utter devotion to him; they rejoice that they are accounted worthy to suffer for him; yet when they are preaching and urging the multitudes to believe in him, they never base their appeals on any description of him, the Lord they had seen and listened to; they never exalt and fortify their converts with the words they had heard him speak. He is quoted in the Acts only twice, two short sentences. There is nothing in the entire book to suggest that apart from his death and resurrection the facts of Christ's life were of any interest to anyone. These men were his apostles and his martyrs, but what he was when he was alive had become unimportant to them.

The only possible explanation for this state of mind is that they were conscious of having such an immediate spiritual relation to the glorified Son of God that they cared for nothing else; they lived day by day as in the presence of him who had risen from the dead. This Christ they knew; they were his followers faithful unto death, as they had not known or been faithful to the Christ who had lived on earth.

But inevitably as the years went on men began to wish to have a permanent record of him. Our actual knowledge stops for many years with the end of the Acts. But we can be sure that in the scattered Christian communities where, it might be, a man who remembered Christ was still alive, and where stories about him and words he had spoken were certainly passed on from one to another who had heard them from his disciples, it could not have failed to occur to some that these memories would in the end be lost if they were not recorded. Indeed we know from St. Luke that this did happen. "Many have taken it in hand,"

49

he says, "to set forth in order those things believed among us."

Of those many the four Gospels alone have come down to us. Why they survived when the others did not we have no information at all, nor just when they were written. They are not specifically mentioned, under the names of their traditional authors, until the second century is well on its way, and the very first mention is a criticism of two of them. It comes from a Bishop Papias before the middle of the second century. He writes: "Mark, having become the interpreter of Peter, wrote down accurately everything he remembered, without, however, recording in order what was said and done by Christ. For he did not hear the Lord nor follow him, but Peter, who had no design of giving a connected account." That is, all Mark says is true, but he has got his facts in the wrong order. A statement about Matthew follows: "So Matthew composed the discourses in the Hebrew language and each one interpreted them as he could." That is, there is no one authorized and completely correct version. About the same time the Christian philosopher, Justin Martyr, mentions as being read in the churches "Memoirs called Gospels," but when he speaks of "the Scriptures," he means only the Old Testament.

Up to the year 150 these are the only direct references to the Gospels which have come down to us. It seems at first sight inexplicable that it should be so. In those earliest days of Christianity marked by such devotion to Christ how could these four records of him, incomparably lofty and beautiful, be passed over in silence. But when all we know about that time is considered, reasons appear.

The Christian world then was full of floating memories of Christ. We should expect this to be so even if there were no proof. What Christ had been would not quickly be dropped from men's minds. But there is proof. Two of the very few writers of the time who have come down to us bear witness how eagerly Christians were talking. Both of them were bishops, responsible men. One was the judicious Papias. He says: "When a person came my way who had been a follower of the Elders, I would inquire what was said by Andrew or Peter or Philip, or Thomas or James or John or Matthew or any other of the Lord's disciples, and what Aristion and the Elder John, the disciples of the Lord, say. For I did not think I could get as much profit from books as from the utterance of a living voice." It is not hard to understand the bishop's preference. There were many living voices then. Some who like "Aristion and the Elder John" could say, "I was there when he said— I saw him do—." More who could repeat what they had heard from Andrew and Philip and the rest. To say these names over is to be reminded of how much was not recorded. We have no "Gospel according to St. Andrew."

Fifty years after Papias another bishop, Irenaeus, wrote to a friend: "I saw thee when I was still a boy in company with Polycarp. I remember what happened there better than events of recent occurrence. I can describe the very place where the blessed Polycarp used to sit, and his personal appearance, and how he would describe his intercourse with John and the rest who had seen the Lord, and how he would relate their words."

Both of these passages give a vivid picture of what Christians then were depending on for their knowledge and their faith. Personal testimonials, information which this and that man had had from those in touch with Christ, these were the important matters. A verse at the end of St. John's Gospel which is held to be a later addition says that if all that Christ did should be written, "I suppose that even the world itself could not contain the books." The words give the impression of a flood of talk, an outpouring of reminiscences, stories, hearsay reports, first- and secondhand experience. What remains of this mass of material is four little books. Three of them to a great extent duplicate each other; together they obviously cover only a minute part of all that information. A verse in the Acts brings vividly to mind what was not recorded. Paul bids his hearers: "Remember the Lord Jesus, how he said, It is more blessed to give than to receive." These words are found nowhere else. Some unknown person heard Christ speak them and repeated them to Paul and so they were saved. Many, many such must have been passed from one man to another and then lost.

The Gospels would make their way slowly in the face of ardent speakers. As Papias said, voices would be set far ahead. Written records could not rival glowing experiences and recollections related by men who had heard those who had heard Christ. And certainly it was not an age of readers. Our two bishops show that all this was true; nevertheless the four survived. Men depended chiefly on verbal accounts of Christ, but what has always been true of the Gospels was true then and was recognized even by those who had heard apostles speak. In them, brief as they were, so much omitted and so much repeated, men of all sorts and all opinions found Christ himself, his very portrait, so drawn that it seemed almost his living presence. There was no danger that they might be swept away by the flood of talk.

But during those years some additions to them must have been made. There was nothing to prevent. They did not yet belong to the class of sacred literature which may not be added to or taken from. No objection would have been felt to putting into them something which in the eyes of the men who had some real perception of what Christ was, could fittingly find a place in the record of him. We can take for granted a reverent regard for truth in that early Christian community, but some of their own cherished convictions would inevitably get in. They would not be on their guard against admitting a belief which they accepted ardently and valued greatly. What was added can be decided only in one way, through Christ himself. Did he utter that scathing denunciation of the Pharisees who taught a lofty morality? Was it like him to choose them out for bitter attack and say nothing about the powerful priestly party who had allowed the temple to be turned into a den of thieves? Did he believe in devils who could get into a herd of swine, or is that tale a bit of black oriental magic such as Rome then was full of, foisted onto the Gospels? He alone can guide us here.

Did he say to his disciples when they went out to preach the kingdom of God, that they must not enter any city of the Samaritans, thus, certainly by implication, banning those heretic Jews from the kingdom, or did he tell the parable about the Samaritan who was neighbour to him that fell among thieves when the priest and the Levite passed by on the other side? He did not say both; it is not hard to decide which he did say. Did he dictate a procedure to be followed "if thy brother shall trespass against thee," which began with telling him privately his fault, then if he was obdurate, calling in witnesses to hear the charge and, if he still did not repent, telling the church and, "if he neglect to hear the church, let him be to thee as a heathen man and a publican?" Or is it true that when Peter asked, "How oft shall my brother sin against me and I forgive him? Until

54

seven times?" Christ said, "I say not unto thee until seven times: but until seventy times seven." We must choose which of these two ways of acting we believe Christ advocated. Here too we might consider whether he who told Peter to have illimitable forgiveness toward him who sinned against him, also said that God would punish with eternal damnation those who sinned against Him, whether he told hotheaded Peter that he must be more forgiving than his Father in heaven.

What we have to do is try to discover the true light, the white radiance behind the many coloured rays through which from the very first it was seen. Nothing except a fixed conviction that the Gospels sprang into being perfect from beginning to end, can be put against the weight of evidence that there is material in them later than the lifetime of Christ.

The example most generally recognized is the last twelve verses of Mark which give a brief résumé rather than an account of the Resurrection, together with a statement that he who does not believe will be damned. A list of the miracles follows which Christ's disciples will perform, among others, handling serpents and drinking poison with immunity. The entire passage is on a level immeasurably below the rest of the Gospel. As early as the fourth century, churchmen held that it was added by some unknown hand when the original ending had been lost, and ever since scholars have agreed.

Another example, which has not been so widely accepted because the idea in it was extremely attractive to Christians, is the statement about the imminent end of the world ascribed to Christ in three Gospels. In Matthew, Mark and Luke, Christ is represented as foretelling frightful calamities which are about to happen, and which will usher in his triumph together with that of all his followers. This, except for the part assigned to Christ, is precisely the belief which had comforted the Hebrews for centuries after they had returned from the captivity in Babylon. In every national disaster they saw the prelude to "the great and dreadful Day of the Lord." They had ceased to be an independent nation and in their helpless subjection what could be so easily convincing and so passionately held as the belief that they need not struggle to deliver themselves; God would take entire charge. He would "burn as stubble" their oppressors and make them the rulers over the earth, freed from the awful responsibility Isaiah and Jeremiah had declared was laid upon men, to bring about themselves the reign of God on earth.

Generation after generation passed and the hope was never fulfilled, yet men loved it so, they would not let it die. In times of peace and prosperity it would be dormant, but when misfortune came it blazed up. An old prophecy would be brought forward as applying not to the time when it was spoken—to which clearly it had not applied —but to the present, or a new prophecy would be put in the mouth of some great man of old. A number of such writings later than the Old Testament have come down to us, the latest just before or just after the birth of Christ. Then, as far as Jewish writings are concerned, there is a long pause. We know of none during Christ's life or for nearly forty years after. It would seem that all that time the hope was in abeyance. Rome had taken the country over and there was comparative tranquility. But later on revolts broke out and civil war, and finally a Roman army captured Jerusalem and destroyed the temple. In the face of that terrible calamity the hope, of course, came to life again. We have many Jewish writings of the time which announce the approaching end of the world and the glorious triumph of Israel.

No writer among the Jews tried to kindle the great expectation during Christ's lifetime. There was no signal disaster which would lead people to turn to it. Yet the first three Gospels all say that even so Christ brought it to life. They ascribe to him a most vivid and detailed account of the destruction of heaven and earth together with the statement, usual in these predictions, that the present generation would not pass away until it took place. The thirteenth chapter of Mark is a perfect example of this kind of writing. Christ is represented as saying that there shall be affliction such as there was not from the beginning; wars and earthquakes and famines; the sun and the moon darkened. Then he himself will come with power and glory and gather his elect from the ends of the earth.

This is the very essence of what had sustained the Jews through their long continued humiliation. The Christian Jews had been brought up in it. Their instinct would be to turn to it when times were hard, and they would of course ascribe the prophecy to Christ, as their forefathers in each case had ascribed theirs to some great leader of old. Tradition says Mark was written about the time of Nero's persecution in Rome when the sufferings of the Christians were terrible. But all the last part of the first century was very hard for them. They were persecuted; their central authority came to an end with the fall of Jerusalem; their great leaders were put to death. The destruction of the temple was as shocking to them as to the orthodox Jews. Nothing could be more natural than for them to revive the ancient hope in a new dress.

Such a conviction, so consoling, so triumphant, could hardly fail to make its way into the records of Christ's life. No doubt those responsible thought they were doing a service to the faith. Authorship received little consideration in the ancient world. If anyone could improve a piece of writing, so much the better. No doubt, too, the Christians would easily persuade themselves that Christ really had so prophesied. At the very least, he who had proclaimed the coming of the kingdom of God, would certainly have approved this declaration of its swift approach. Here was all-sufficient comfort for the Christians in their poverty and obscurity and ever-threatening danger. In a very little while their persecutors would be destroyed and they themselves would reign gloriously forever. Small wonder that this glowing belief was with the most pious intentions added to the Gospels.

This is not mere conjecture. In the Acts, which opens directly after Christ's ascension, there is not a word about the great hope except in one sentence which ends a quotation from an Old Testament prophecy. If Christ's disciples were convinced that the end of the world was at hand together with the triumphant reign of the Christians, they had a tremendously strong ground for appealing to the people they were trying to convert. It would be a most singular fact if the Christian leaders had held this catastrophic belief and never encouraged believers or threatened unbelievers with it. But in the whole of Acts it is only once mentioned, when Peter repeats some words of the prophet Joel which end with a reference to the day of the Lord. It is not alluded to again, unless the phrase in the third chapter, "the times of restitution of all things," is an obscure reference to it. If the awful words in Mark had really been spoken by Christ, as reported, in circumstances of great solemnity just before his death, it is inconceivable that the first Christians never referred to them.

The only possible conclusion is that Christ did not speak them. Granted that the idea of such a thrilling triumph was irresistibly alluring to the despised and hard-pressed early Christians, it is astonishing that the church could continue to ascribe it to Christ. The point of view involved, that there could be a triumph of the righteousness he would have people seek, forgiveness and compassion and humility and love, brought about by the darkening of the heavens and the destruction of the earth and the wiping out of the wicked—all this is so utterly foreign to him, is, indeed, so utterly foreign to what constitutes a moral triumph, that one is lost in wonder that a single person ever believed it of him. The greatest Hebrew prophets would have rejected it no less.

The fact that it was ascribed to him is another example of how easily incompatibles are accepted. The Sermon on the Mount would be irrelevant in a world that was on the point of coming to an end.

We have to keep in mind the difference between those times and our own. The evangelists were men of their day. It would never occur to them that what was taken for granted by everyone Christ might reject. We cannot look at him only through their eyes; we must use our own. If Christ is here for the modern world, it is because he is independent of changes of time and stages of knowledge. Today it is impossible to find a refuge from the evils of the world in an expectation that presently God will intervene to destroy the wicked

60

and exalt the good. The same thing is true of miracles ascribed to Christ. They belong to the days when the Gospels were taking shape, not to our day. Then the world was given over to magic. Even hard-headed Rome had been invaded by dark oriental mysteries and marvels. In the Gospels the attitude seems to be not that miracles are a stupendous, awesome occurrence, but rather that they are to be expected. Christ is repeatedly asked to perform them. "A sign!" the people clamour. "Give us a sign." No one then could have been believed in as coming from God without the backing of marvels.

At the very beginning of his public life Christ set his face against signs and wonders. In the wilderness the idea came to him of using his great powers to perform spectacular deeds, and he rejected it. He would have no traffic with wonder-working. And yet the gospel record declares that later he departed from this resolution. He performed, we are told, many marvels, some motivated by compassion, as when he fed thousands of hungry people with a few loaves and fishes, but others designed to exhibit his power, as when he healed a palsied man in order to prove to the skeptical crowd watching him, so St. Luke reports him as saying "that the Son of Man hath power to forgive sins," and when he drove out devils from a man into a herd of swine and bade him go and proclaim to his friends "how great things the Lord hath done for thee." There is a direct contradition here. In the wilderness he turned decisively away from showing how great things he could do. The idea that he could make use of a marvelous deed to bring about good was just what he cast behind him in the second temptation. Is it credible that he returned to it later? The conviction that no wonderful, inexplicable act could prove truth or bring about good, which had carried him through the temptations, shines out unmistakably again and again later in the Gospels. Often he heals a man and bids him, "See thou tell no one." He will not have men's belief in him depend upon marvelous cures. To Thomas who insisted that he would accept the truth only if he saw and touched it, Christ said, "Blessed are they which have not seen and yet have believed."

There are two contradictory accounts of him in the Gospels. He who said in one of his rare moments of anger, "An evil and adulterous generation seeketh for a sign. There shall no sign be given them," who "sighed deeply in his spirit and said, Except ye see signs and wonders ye will in no wise believe," is also represented as working signs and wonders to make men believe. One of the two is true; both cannot be. No one has ever seen in Christ an uncertain mind, wavering between opposites or capable of embracing both at once.

There is a tale in St. Matthew about how Peter came to Christ for money to pay the state tax and how Christ bade him go fishing and open the mouth of the first fish he caught where he would find the required sum. There is something shocking in a story like this placed in the pure and piercing atmosphere of the Gospels and in face of the majesty of the presence of Christ. That is true, if in a less degree, of a number of the miracles. They were added to the Gospels by men who had heard of his glory from those who had beheld it. Perhaps they knew of no other way to show the world how glorious he was. Magic was the one irrefutable proof of God's favour. Without it Christ would be an impostor and they knew he was not. They never had an idea what they did to him in showing him to the world as "a man approved of God among you by miracles and signs and wonders."

And yet hundreds of years before, the Hebrews had had a long line of great religious teachers who claimed to be the mouthpiece of God and did no miracles. From Isaiah on, the prophets delivered their message, "Thus saith the Lord," and were accepted as God's messengers without any wonders to vouch for them. With a single exception, magical tales were not told about them. Only once the record of their mighty summons to men for justice and mercy was enfeebled by a wonder-working story. Amos did not call down fire from heaven upon the wicked rich. Hosea's wife was not led back to him by an angel. Jeremiah was not delivered from the miry dungeon by a chariot from heaven. The earlier prophets had been magicians. Iron floated on the water for them; a jar of oil remained always full; the dead were brought back to life. But Amos came and all that sort of thing stopped. We do not have to try to free the great prophets from magical coverings in order to see them clearly. Those who recorded them kept them free, as did also those who preserved the record. Extraordinarily, no one attempted to support the truth of their words by telling wonders about them. It is as if there had been a general recognition that what they said was its own evidence.

There is no way to know why this was so and why when the Gospels were being written it was no longer so. Christ was in the direct line of descent from these greatest Hebrews and their way of convincing men that they spoke God's truth was his way. He showed in a single sentence what he thought about wonder-working as a proof of the truth. In the parable of Dives and Lazarus, when Dives prays Abraham to send Lazarus to his brothers to recall them from their evil ways, Abraham tells him, "They have Moses and the prophets; let them hear them." Dives cries out, "Nay, but if one went to them from the dead, they will repent." Abraham answers, "If they hear not Moses and the prophets, neither will they be persuaded though one rose from the dead." In that one brief sentence Christ dismissed the supernatural as evidence of the truth. No miracle, even the most wonderful, the resurrection of the

64

dead, would mean anything as a guarantee that what the prophets said was true—or that what he himself said was true. Spiritual truth must be its own proof. But he alone in his generation saw that the spiritual cannot be proved by the supernatural.

We have not yet begun to realize his stature. He towers high above magic and all its works. To see him in some degree as he was, to perceive something of his unsurpassable greatness which forever soars beyond our comprehension and yet continually lifts us up toward him, we must strip magic away. Only when it is set aside can we catch a glimpse of Christ himself, attended by his own miracles, the miracle of what he was and the miracle that the world, antagonistic to him, opposed to all he taught, has yet never been able to forget him and let him go. These are the signs and wonders which through all the generations testify of him.

The officers sent to arrest him said, "Never man spake like this man." He spoke the truth as no else ever spoke it. What men wanted from him was magic.

IV

How the Gospels Became
the Word of God

Jesus Christ the same yesterday, and today, and forever.
—Hebrews 13:8

IN BISHOP PAPIAS' day the Gospels were writings anyone, even a church dignitary, could pick flaws in. Not more than fifty years later they were fully accepted as the Word of God. That was around the year 180 when Irenaeus, the bishop who had listened as a boy to Polycarp, wrote: "Matthew published his written Gospel among the Hebrews while Peter and Paul were preaching and founding the church in Rome. After their death Mark, the disciple and interpreter of Peter, transmitted to us in writing those things which Peter had preached; and Luke, the attendant of Paul, recorded in a book the Gospel which Paul had declared. (The tradition was that Luke had gained his knowledge of Christ's life from Paul who in his own writings paid little or no attention to it.) Afterwards John, the disciple of the Lord who also reclined on his bosom, published the Gospel while residing at Ephesus. It is impossible that the Gospels should be either more or fewer than these. For since there are four regions in the world and four principal winds, so the Gospels are the church's ground and breath of life. And the Cherubim hath four faces and the Living Creatures are quadriform, so the Gospel is quadriform." Whatever may be thought of the argument, it proves at any rate that by that time the authority of the Gospels was beyond question. But how this came about in the thirty years or so, perhaps less, between Justin and Irenaeus, both of whom taught in Rome, what the intermediate steps were between Papias the critical and Irenaeus the wholehearted believer, we have almost no information. To Justin they were not holy scripture. Some years after Justin we have a Harmony of the Four which shows by implication that they were growing in importance, but there is no direct mention of them until Irenaeus speaks of them as the flawless work of God. It seems an extraordinarily quick transformation, but if we try to put ourselves back into that half century or so about which so little has come down to us, some reasons for the swift change appear.

Christ was a new figure in the world. Nothing like him had ever been known. Even so, it was easy to be sure how he would have men act. The Christian Way was quite clear to the first Christians.

They were uncertain about some matters, whether, for instance, they should keep the Jewish law about food or about circumcision, but there is not a hint in the Acts that they were ever uncertain about how they ought to live to please Christ. This they knew and never questioned. But to live so as to please Christ was a strenuous method of forwarding Christ's cause, and of course the time came when to argue about him and to explain him was held to be as praiseworthy as to imitate him. But while it was easy to know how to follow him, it was not easy to understand him. So men began to explain him in different ways.

Early in the second century one explanation was made which in the end attracted a great deal of attention and convinced many Christians. It was attractive because it explained that always most disturbing problem, the existence of evil. There were two Gods, according to this theology, one evil, the creator of the world, the other good, made manifest in Christ who was all spirit and had no part in evil matter. He did not really die on the cross. He left his body there, which, indeed, had not been an actual body, and departed to heaven. All attention to material things, "the service of the perishable," must be avoided by Christians as far as possible. St. Paul's low opinion of marriage was strengthened into what often amounted to a prohibition of it. The advocates of this doctrine declared that Christ's apostles had not understood him, but St. Paul had and also

71

St. Luke, his pupil. St. Paul's Epistles and the
Gospel of St. Luke were the Word of God, a solid
support Christians could depend upon. There
was much in Paul which could be urged to con-
firm this point of view and of course the passages
which went against it could be dropped. Luke's
close connection with Paul accounts for his Gospel
having been the one chosen.

We have definite information that in later days
strong opposition arose to this teaching, but we
do not need it to be sure that from the very beginning it violently antagonized the Christian
Jews. It went directly against the basic Hebrew
belief that there was one God of perfect righteousness who had created matter. That idea was fundamental in Jewish thought. No Jew ever looked at
matter as evil. The Jews turned Christian must
have fought with all their strength a teaching
which degraded the body, but they must have
felt their need of some written authority to support them, such as their opponents declared they
had. St. Paul and St. Luke together were formid-
able and the question at stake was very important.
The belief that Christ actually lived a human life
had far-reaching implications. What was involved
was nothing less than the Incarnation, the belief
that the divine could dwell in the human. Just
when this fundamental Christian doctrine was
strongly attacked the Gospels emerged from a
position where they were critically considered
into one of full authority as the Word of God. No

support can be found in them of the contempt and hatred of the body, which has always worked evil when admitted to a religion. The whole tenor of Christ's life was against the idea that the mortification of the flesh was good in itself or that self-inflicted pain could be the service of God. Hard as his life and death were, he never held up suffering as a good to be sought.

It is more than reasonable, it is most probable, that the Gospels were given their sudden preeminence by those who were struggling to keep Christ upon the earth a man among men, to prevent him from becoming wholly an ineffable spiritual mystery. In this light the strange insistence in the Gospel of St. Luke that Christ's body after the resurrection was not "spirit," but "flesh and bones," becomes comprehensible, as also the story of his eating "a piece of broiled fish, and of an honeycomb." The ardent advocates of his humanity felt that they had to emphasize it—and in the very Gospel chosen by their opponents—even to the point of suggesting that the life after death was dependent upon food.

With the pronouncement that all four were the very Word of God a freezing period set in, exactly as had happened in the case of the Old Testament. Not an alteration was possible. During the years when they were being added to, no attempt had been made to do away with the differences between them. It is reasonable to suppose that at first each of the four was in a different part of the world and was accepted as the one and only Gospel of Christ. Later on when all were available, Justin Martyr's attitude toward them, that they did not belong to holy scripture, points to their not yet being important enough to be carefully compared and revised. But that was a state of things which would not have lasted long.

They were written during the most individualistic, the least standardized, period in the history of Christianity, when there was no authority anywhere to bring into line what men remembered about Christ and see to it that nothing was said in Ephesus which did not agree with what was said in Rome. The wonder is not that there were differences between them when they were written, but that the most evident contradictions, at the very least, were not done away with later, before every word was declared to have come from God. Nothing would seem easier than for the churchmen toward the end of the second century to have constructed a clear consistent narrative of Christ's life on the basis of the Gospels. But the truth must be that it was not easy. Otherwise it would have been done. The explanation often given, and it seems reasonable, is that by the time Christians had to have a documentary support, they were confronted with four Gospels which had to be taken as they were because each was the venerated possession of a church too powerful to be offended or ignored, Mark of Rome,

John of Ephesus, Matthew of some great city in Palestine, and Luke in Greece.

At all events, whether in this way or another, it came about that there were four records, not one. If the early church had worked the Gospels over, no doubt all difficulties would have been eliminated and Christians ever since would have had an easier time, but the result would have been something standardized and brought into an imposed agreement, a kind of mass production. It would be our immense loss if we had only one impeccable life of Christ, discrepancies all smoothed away, every part accurately fitted into the whole. The separate accounts, each with marked characteristics, prove as a single one never could that Christ lived and walked this earth, an actual personality. The differences are extraordinarily illuminating. Far from being a trouble, they are altogether an advantage. We have four accounts written from four separate points of view, but we have only one Christ. He is the same in them all.

V

The Gospels

But we have this treasure in earthen vessels.

—II Corinthians 4:7

THE ONLY SOURCE of our knowledge about Christ himself is the Gospels. The rest of the New Testament has to do with the result of his life, the experiences of his first followers. St. Paul, who wrote a large part of it and is by far the most important of the writers, gave very little thought to the Christ who had lived in Palestine. He had never known him. What he cared about was the Christ of his own inner conviction who had appeared to him in a vision. His great concern was to show what Christ was to him. The gospels are singularly unlike this personal history. The men responsible for them never occupy the foreground for a moment. Something of what they were comes through, of course, their point of view, their convictions, but not of set purpose. They say nothing about them-selves; they never comment upon their own reactions to Christ. It is the reverse of St. Paul's method. We are on intimate terms with St. Paul; but we can see only dimly the men who have given us the most important part of the Bible. They recorded Christ; as far as they could they left themselves out.

They were editors rather than authors. The gospels they wrote were based not upon their own firsthand knowledge, but upon information they had gathered from others. None of them ever came into contact with Christ. That has always been accepted as true of Luke and Mark, who do not appear in the gospels, but it is equally true of the authors of Matthew and John. It is proved by the fact that they both made use of Mark. The Gospel of Matthew, indeed, includes almost all of Mark, sometimes reproducing his very words. The apostle Matthew had lived with Christ; he had his own personal impressions of him. He would never have turned to Mark for information. The same thing is true of the Gospel of John. It includes much less of Mark; the writer uses him only a little, but the fact that he uses him at all is conclusive against his being the apostle who of all Christ's disciples had the closest relation to him. He would not have gone to another for any of his material, above all to someone who had not known Christ.

The men who collected the earliest records and reports and made the gospels from them have not left us so much as their names. A verse toward the end of John says it was written by "the disciple whom Jesus loved," but he is nameless. Also the scholars say that that part of the gospel is a later addition. Luke is addressed to a Roman who knew without being told who the man writing to him was. Matthew and Mark give no indication of who they were. The second century was nearing its close before names were attached to all four. It would be very natural for a later age when it had become important to assert the authority of the gospels to declare that apostles were their authors. The only cause for surprise is that they did not do so to all four. Matthew is not a prominent apostle, but it was easy to ascribe a gospel to him because, as Papias said, Matthew wrote down "discourses" of Christ. The case for John of course was still easier. It rested on accepting as belonging to the original gospel the statement about its having been written by the disciple Jesus loved, always identified as John.

Mark and Luke were familiar figures to the early church. Both had been companions of Paul and both had been with him during his last days in prison. Mark too was known to have had a close connection with Peter. If they had not the rank of apostles themselves, they had the support of friendship with the two greatest apostles and their gospels were never held to be less authoritative than those ascribed to Matthew and John.

Mark, Papias said, had but one authority for his gospel. He wrote down what Peter told him "accurately," following Peter in all respects. Papias' date as a writer is estimated as not earlier than 115 and not later than 140, so that he lived fairly close to the time when the Gospel was written. That, according to Irenaeus, was after Peter and Paul had died, which it is generally supposed took place during Nero's persecution of the Christians in 64. Even if Mark wrote his gospel soon after, Papias was separated from it by less than seventy years on the highest estimate. That is fairly early testimony and carries weight. It is not necessary to assume that Mark put nothing into the gospel which he did not get from Peter. No one's word except Mark's could be accepted on such a point and Mark never said anything. But we can conclude that Peter was Mark's chief authority and that his spirit and his point of view prevailed.

It seems beyond dispute therefore that none of the four gospels is the work of a man who wrote down what he himself knew from his own knowledge of Christ. Mark depended on Peter; each of the other three depended partly on Mark, partly on other sources. All of them had at least one private source known to him alone. The completely different stories Matthew and Luke tell about the birth of Christ are a case in point. Each of them had come upon an account which the other had never heard, or, perhaps, which he rejected in favour of the one he preferred.

The four evangelists should be looked upon as

editors, not authors. From this point of view Mark is the most important. His edition of Christ's life was the first. Matthew and Luke re-edited him; John, whose main sources were different from those used by the other three, still made use of him.

1. The Gospel of Mark

THE GOSPEL OF MARK is a very surprising document. The author is reasonably supposed to be the Mark who is mentioned a number of times in the Acts of the Apostles and whom Paul summoned to Rome when he was in prison there. "Do thy diligence to come shortly unto me," Paul writes to Timothy. "Take Mark and bring him with thee." Mark then was with Paul during the last days of his life, and must have known well what Paul thought about Christ and Christianity. Even without the close personal relationship he would have known, for Paul had begun to write his epistles years before his imprisonment and they must have been widely circulated among Christians by the time Mark started writing. It is difficult to think of Paul with his extraordinary endowments and his faith at once passionate and clearly reasoned, not exercising a controlling influence over a young man, as Mark was then. Yet Mark in writing his gospel turned completely away from him. The gospel is as un-

like the epistles as two documents about Christ
could be.

The Christian world had in the writings of
Paul a clear explanation of that crucial problem,
the existence of evil, a clear statement of what
God's plan for mankind was and the part assigned to Christ in it, and clarity and definiteness
in religion have a very strong attraction. Nevertheless when Mark undertook to write Christ's
life, he discarded everything Paul had said. He
did not do so in favour of a different explanation.
He gave up Paul's theology, but he did not sub-
stitute another. He gave no explanations at all;
he did not say who Christ was or why he came
or why he died.

His point of view, the way he looks at Christ,
is just what Peter emphasizes in his speeches in
the Acts. When Peter says to the centurion,
"How God anointed Jesus of Nazareth with the
Holy Spirit and with power; who went about doing good and healing all that were oppressed by
the devil; for God was with him" the matter-of-
fact statement might be a summary of Mark's
creed.

But the gospel is not only surprising theologi-
cally. Along with this lack of wanting to explain
Christ, which gives the impression that the writer
is a practical man who cares above all for facts,
there is an interest in miraculous stories which
makes all else that Christ does—and says—of

84

quite secondary importance. Back of this picture of Christ the wonder-worker, there is another picture of him, but it is so overshadowed by the first, that it is hard to see and must be sought for. Mark gives far more space proportionately to miracles than any of the three other evangelists. Of course he did not attempt to account for them. He would not have felt any need to do so. In those days there was nothing improbable, so to speak, about supernatural wonders. They were comprehensible events, the proofs naturally to be expected of God's special approval.

Mark had just the kind of simple, objective mind that would take to marvels, or perhaps it was Peter that had it. Mark's gospel was due first of all to Peter, and clearly Peter did not share Paul's need to explain Christ. He had lived with him as Paul had not. He had listened to him, watched him, walked the roads with him. He had felt the power of his living presence. That was what he wanted to leave with Mark, not explanations. Christ had not been given to making them. Occasionally he had told his disciples the meaning of a parable, but for the most part he let them wonder. "They understood not that saying and were afraid to ask him." "They feared exceedingly and said one to another, What manner of man is this?" "They were sore amazed in themselves beyond measure, and wondered." Sometimes Christ had wondered too. "And he said unto them, How is it that ye do not understand?" But they had to learn for themselves; he would not tell them.

Strange though it seems with all his love of the marvelous there is in Mark no miraculous birth. No wise men come to adore the child; no angels sing his praise; no prophets foretell his glory. He appears first at his baptism with this introduction only, "Jesus Christ, the Son of God." His family, his birthplace, all his life up to that moment, are passed over as of no importance. Christ's warrant is not that he is the king who should be born in Bethlehem of David's royal line, as in Luke, nor the Messiah, God's anointed, who should set the Jews in triumph over their enemies, as in Matthew. He receives his warrant at his baptism: he is the Son of God. "And there came a voice from heaven saying, Thou art my beloved Son in whom I am well pleased."

Only a single verse is given to the temptation, and then Mark says, "Jesus came into Galilee preaching the gospel of the kingdom of God, and saying, The time is fulfilled, and the kingdom of God is at hand: repent ye and believe the gospel." Christ came to summon men to the kingdom. There is not a word anywhere in Mark to indicate that Christ thought of himself as the centre of his teaching. He sends his disciples out on a mission, but not to tell men about him. "They preached that men should repent." Neither does Christ say that he alone can show the way to the kingdom. There are "the righteous who need no repentance"; presumably it lies open to them. "They that are whole have no need of the physician." Christ's mission is to open it to the others, the sinners, the outcast, the despised, the lost.

In this gospel the tone of lofty authority is absent, such as there is in Matthew's "Ye have heard that it hath been said by them of old, but I say unto you," and in Luke's, "He that denieth me before men shall be denied before the angels of God." There is nothing in Mark to set beside such statements. In Matthew when Peter says that he is the Messiah, Christ praises him: "Blessed art thou, for flesh and blood hath not revealed it to thee, but my Father which is in heaven." In Mark, in Peter's gospel, the story is given a completely different turn. Christ refuses to be identified as the Messiah. Peter is not praised. Christ "rebuked" his disciples, and told them that nothing could be further from the Messianic triumph than the life that lay before him and those who followed him. "He began to teach them that the Son of Man must suffer many things," and "Whosoever will come after me, let him deny himself, and take up his cross, and follow me."

It is true that twice in Mark Christ declares that he is the Messiah; at least he says that he will come in the glory of his Father with the holy angels, clearly a description of the advent of the triumphant Messiah, but a contradiction that is found in only two verses is not important. They could so easily have been added, just as the chapter about the end of the world could have been added after the temple was burned and the Messiah expected at any moment. Nowhere else in the gospel does Christ claim a lofty position for himself or allow his disciples to do so. He never calls himself the Son of God, only the Son of man.

Not Luke, but both Matthew and John try to fit him into a scheme or a theory they have made. Mark has never such an idea. He is bent only on telling what Christ did and said. His authorities left many gaps. Much of Christ's greatest teaching is not in Mark. He gives only two or three of the sayings in the Sermon on the Mount. It would seem that Peter had not thought them important, or most of the parables either. Often Mark says, "Jesus preached the word to them and many hearing him were astonished"; "They were astonished at his doctrine"; but he does not say why they were astonished, what the doctrine and the words were. The kingdom of God is emphasized throughout the gospel; Mark returns to it again and again, but even so, his real interest is not in what Christ said, but in what he did.

Mark was a storyteller, not a thinker. It would seem that that too was Peter's turn of mind. What he had heard Christ say for the most part failed to catch his attention. But the cures Christ wrought and the way he could calm distracted minds were matters for veneration and delight never to be forgotten; they were all vividly portrayed in the picture he painted for Mark. In the years that followed Christ's death the wonders were multiplied, as always happens to wonders. To Mark, Christ was above all a worker of marvels, endowed with illimitable power, who raised the dead, whom the elements obeyed and demons feared and voices from heaven acclaimed.

This supernatural Being occupies all the foreground of the gospel. There is hardly a chapter in which a miracle is not performed—or two or three. Only far in the background another figure can be seen, the Son of man, who made no claim for himself, who pointed men not to himself, but to the kingdom of God. This personage was not superior to the laws of nature; he got tired and was troubled; he was "greatly amazed" and "exceedingly sorrowful"; he prayed in anguish that he might not have to suffer death on the cross.

The teaching Mark records seems to belong to him only. It has nothing to do with the miraculous. The kingdom of God in which it centred, far from being ushered in by marvels, was like that quiet hidden process, the growth of the seed down in the earth up into the blade and the ear and the full corn in the ear. No miracle could bring it to pass nor could it be found by a miracle. Only those could enter it who were at the farthest remove from manifestations of extraordinary powers and strange awesome doings, the humble of spirit, those willing to be lowest of all. Throughout Mark there is this sharp contrast, spectacular wonders on one side, used sometimes to solve difficulties, to calm a dangerous storm or reach a boat far from land, and on the other side the most unspectacular, the most realistic and difficult, solution to the enigma of human life.

Mark never attempted to bring these two pictures of Christ together.

2. The Gospel of Matthew

THE GOSPEL OF MATTHEW is the Gospel of Mark with additions. Almost all of Mark is repeated in Matthew. A good deal of Christ's teaching is added, notably the Sermon on the Mount, together with a beginning and an end, an account of Christ's birth and his appearances after his resurrection, but the main part comes from Mark, sometimes in the very words Mark used.

Nevertheless, although Matthew follows Mark, he does so with a difference. The two gospels are quite unlike. Matthew's additions change the whole spirit. He was a devout Jew turned Christian and there is a marked Jewish slant in his gospel, a disposition absent from Mark. In Matthew when Christ sends his disciples forth to teach, he bids them avoid the Samaritan heretics, hateful to Jews: "Into any city of the Samaritans enter ye not." They are to go only to "the lost sheep of Israel," to whom alone Christ declares he has been sent. Not one word of this is in the corresponding passage in Mark. Again, Mark gives a great saying of Christ's which makes human welfare the test of religious practice, "The Sabbath was made for man, and not man for the Sabbath." Matthew takes over the incident which drew forth Christ's words, but he does not give the saying. It would have been intolerable to him as a Jew, to whom the due observance of the Sabbath was indubitably one chief reason for man's existence. He does give the feeble and completely illogical conclusion drawn by Mark, but certainly never spoken by Christ, "Therefore the Son of man is Lord also of the Sabbath." This constituted a tremendous claim to Christ's supremacy in the eyes of a Jew, and Matthew gladly recorded it. It was in line with the way he wished to present Christ to the Christian Jews. He was their spokesman. He brought together into one the two contradictory pictures in Mark and fitted it into the framework of the Jewish mind of the day.

The Jews saw the world against a background of tremendous expectations and triumphant hopes inherited through generations and fixed by education and association until they could hardly be changed. For a Jew to become a follower of Christ was much more difficult than for a Greek or a Roman. There was only one way in which he could be acceptable to Jews, if he was seen as the fulfillment of the ages-old expectation of the nation, the one sent from God to deliver God's people. When Matthew was brought into contact with Christ through those who had known him and written of him, who had felt the power of his presence and were assured that he had the words of eternal life, he looked at this strange and overpowering personality he was compelled to revere, in the light of his own deeply rooted hopes. Christ was the Deliverer whom Israel had been waiting for through hundreds of years. He was the Messiah, the Anointed, an ancient title given to the kings of old which had acquired a very different and a very definite meaning in the centuries since Old Testament days.

The Jews did not put their golden age of peace and plenty in the past as the Greeks and Romans did, but in the future. Seven hundred years before Christ Isaiah had foretold the coming of a son of David who would judge with righteousness and establish his government upon the throne of David forever, and the later prophets took up the theme. Sometimes it was a descendent of David who would bring about the triumph of God's people, sometimes the Lord God Himself would intervene. The usual prelude was the great and dreadful Day of the Lord, cruel with wrath and fierce anger, when the wicked would be destroyed.

During the centuries between the end of the
Old Testament and the birth of Christ, a strange
type of literature developed from this expectation. A number of the writings have come down
to us, extraordinary productions, awesome visions
and horrible imaginings, bloodthirsty hopes of
vengeance and promises of lofty good, all
jumbled together as in the Book of Revelation, a
true descendent. The golden age was still in the
future, but it was a near future. The Deliverer
was always just at hand. In the Book of Enoch,
parts of which go back to the end of the second
century before Christ, a Holy and Elect One
shall come to deliver the righteous and punish
the wicked. Nothing is said about his being a
descendent of David or occupying an earthly
throne. On the contrary, "Before the sun was
created his name was named before the Lord of
Spirits." God declares that He will give the rulers
of the earth into his hands, "the hands of mine
Elect. As straw in the fire so shall they burn before
the face of the holy, and no trace of them shall
any more be found. . . . And the Elect One
shall in those days sit upon my throne . . . the
Son of Man sitting on the throne of his glory."
He will hand over the wicked "to the angels for
punishment and his sword is drunk with their
blood. . . . And their faces shall be filled with
darkness and shame before the Son of Man. . . .
Be hopeful, ye righteous, for suddenly the sinners shall perish before you and ye shall have

lordship over them according to your desires."

This is a fair example of these strange writings which were one of the chief products of the Jewish mind for some hundreds of years before the birth of Christ. One of them found its way into the Old Testament. In the Book of Daniel, written about the time of the earlier parts of Enoch, there are passages stamped with the same spirit: "One like the Son of man came with the clouds of heaven. . . . And there was given him dominion and glory and a kingdom. . . . The saints of the most High shall take the kingdom and possess the kingdom forever, even forever and ever. . . . And there shall be a time of trouble such as never was since there was a nation even to that same time: and at that time thy people shall be delivered." When the gospel of Matthew was being written "trouble such as never was" had come. The house of the Lord had been burned; the city of the Lord was in the hands of the enemies of the Lord's people. Surely the coming of One like the Son of man, the Holy and Elect One, could not be delayed. No Jewish or Jewish–Christian writing of that particular time could have failed to express some of these ideas. In the Jewish literature that sprang up as soon as the Romans captured Jerusalem they are all expressed. The best known of them represents the writer asking the angel Uriel how long the Jews will be desolate, and why they do not possess the world since the world was made for them,

and the angel answers that very soon they will do
so. He describes the swift and glorious coming of
the Messiah who will destroy Israel's enemies and
set the righteous in perfect blessedness over the
Messianic kingdom.

To the Jews, the Romans were speedily to burn
as straw in the fire and Israel have lordship over
the earth; to Matthew and the Christian Jews,
Christ was the Elect One of God, who had been
crucified, indeed, but would return at any moment, certainly before the death of the present
generation, and inaugurate his reign, deliver up
the wicked to punishment and make the saints
triumph. A number of such statements are in
Matthew. Christ is represented as telling his disciples that they shall not all pass away or taste
of death or even go over the cities of Israel before
they see him coming in his kingdom in the clouds
of heaven, in his glory, in the glory of his Father
with his angels, sitting on the throne of his glory,
on the right hand of power; his disciples on
twelve thrones judging the twelve tribes of Israel.

In accordance with this expected triumph, the
Gospel of Matthew shows that long before his
baptism, even before his birth, Christ was marked
out from all mankind, not only as in Mark at the
baptism. He is "born king of the Jews," the wise
men say to Herod. Matthew traces his genealogy
through the most august personages of Hebrew
history to David and beyond in order to make it
clear that he fulfills the prophecies of what the

Deliverer of Israel would be. The prophets had foretold his descent from David, his birth in "Bethlehem of Judea," the flight to Egypt, too, even little details of his life. Again and again Matthew says that Christ acted thus and so, lived in Nazareth, went to Capernaum, healed the sick, taught in parables, "that it might be fulfilled which was spoken of by the prophets."

This descendent of David, the legal inheritor of David's throne, was very unlike Enoch's Elect One who was created before the sun, but Matthew did not distinguish between them. Christ was both of them, David's son and heir who would sit on David's throne and judge for God's chosen people, and the Son of man who would sit on the throne of his glory and be judge of all men.

The Christian church eagerly took over the idea. The Jews presently gave up the hope of the Messiah, but the Christians never. How much of a part it played in the cruelties the church came to allow and enjoin it is impossible to say, but Enoch's Elect One whose sword is drunk with blood is the same as the Lamb in the Book of Revelation in whose presence the wicked shall be tormented with fire and brimstone. The glorification of ruthless power in the name of Christ was started on its way.

When Christ was seen in this light the miracles were manifestations of supremacy proper to the Messiah. The gap in Mark was closed. The accounts of them must have been a great reassurance to the Jewish Christians for whom Matthew spoke, and they needed it, because Christ's life and teaching went so directly against the exaltation of power, Messianic or not, they were so completely at variance with the picture of the triumphant ruler, that the identification needed a great deal of backing. This Matthew's gospel gave. He saw Christ as every Christian Jew wished to see him after the awful destruction of God's city and God's temple, and he set him forth thus to the Christian–Jewish world.

Nevertheless he would not hold to his thesis when an authority he had found and trusted reported words of Christ which seemed to go against it. Matthew is pre-eminently the evangelist of the Sermon on the Mount, and in this longest and by far most important of Christ's talks recorded by the first three evangelists, there is not a word which could possibly apply to the speaker's being the Messiah. The whole implication is against the idea. Christ hardly mentions himself. He speaks, it is true, with great authority: "Ye have heard that it hath been said by them of old . . . but I say unto you"; nevertheless the centre of the Sermon is God and the kingdom of God. Christ is talking of one thing only, what men must do to do the will of God and so bring about the kingdom. He says nothing about what they must believe. "Ye shall know them by their fruits. Do men gather grapes of thorns, or figs of thistles?" These words are only in Matthew, the Hebrew evangelist. If the fruit is good, the root is good. That sense of the pre-eminent importance of the fruit was a great conception the Jews gave to the world. "He that worketh righteousness is accepted of God." They were tolerant of opinions, but in the realm of conduct there must be a strict following of the narrow way. All the Hebrew in Matthew responded to what Christ said in the Sermon even though the position Christ took in it was inconsistent with his ardent Messianic hopes. He alone of the evangelists put the whole of it into his gospel. There were words in it which must have greatly perplexed and distressed him, but he faithfully set them down. "Resist not evil" has been preserved for us only through Matthew.

In his gospel the picture of Christ drawn by Mark is greatly heightened and added to. He had found the Sermon in an account of Christ which was known to Luke, but unknown to Mark, and in that same account Christ spoke of himself as he did not in Mark's authority or authorities. The personal note is almost completely absent from Mark's gospel. Christ hardly puts forward any claim as regards himself. Once he says that he who gives a cup of cold water in his name shall be rewarded, and he speaks of a man leaving house and brethren and losing his life "for my sake and the gospel's," and declares that he will be ashamed of "whosoever shall be ashamed of

me and my words," but that is all. In the record
Matthew had found, Christ made great claims
upon his followers. He said to his disciples: "Ye
shall be brought before governors and kings for
my sake . . . And ye shall be hated of all men
for my name's sake . . . Whosoever therefore
shall confess me before men, him will I confess
also before my Father which is in heaven . . .
He that loveth father and mother more than me
is not worthy of me . . . And he that taketh not
his cross, and followeth after me, is not worthy of
me . . . He that loseth his life for my sake shall
find it." These sayings have nothing in common
with the claims made for the Elect One of God
and for the Messiah generally, but when they
were placed in Matthew's gospel it was easy to
interpret them as in harmony with the Messianic
idea.

Peter is not rebuked in Matthew as in Mark
for saying that Christ is God's Anointed, but
highly commended. Peter's full statement in Matthew is, "Thou art the Christ, the Son of the living God." In Mark, Christ is chiefly the Son of
man, in Matthew chiefly the Son of God. When
Christ walks on the sea Mark says the disciples
"were sore amazed in themselves beyond measure and wondered," but in Matthew they "worshipped him, saying, Of a truth thou art the Son
of God."

One little detail marks the difference between
the two. In Mark the disciples always address

Christ as Teacher, but in Matthew, with the single exception of Judas on the night of the betrayal, they call him Lord. Even when Matthew is following Mark closely he changes the humbler title to the grander. It was a very lofty title. The Greek translators of the Old Testament used it of God.

Christ has the first place in Matthew. In Mark that place is given to the kingdom of God. Nevertheless Matthew took over almost all that Mark said of the kingdom and added still more. It was the leaven hidden in the meal, the treasure a man will give his all for, the pearl of great price, and "Whosoever therefore shall humble himself as this little child, the same is greatest in the kingdom of heaven." This is very far from the kingdom elsewhere described in his gospel, to be ushered in by the Son of man sitting on the throne of his glory and his disciples on twelve thrones. The other kingdom spreads silently and in hidden ways, and there are no thrones there, but the greatest is the servant of all. Both ideas Matthew set down, carefully and in detail.

Only in his gospel Christ says: "Come unto me, all ye that labour and are heavy laden, and I will give you rest. Take my yoke upon you and learn of me; for I am meek and lowly in heart: and ye shall find rest unto your souls." No doubt Matthew had never a suspicion of the illimitable distance between these words and the picture of the triumphant Son of God and his angels. Was the reason for his confusion Christ himself? Matthew tried to explain him as he wished to see him, but what Christ had actually been, the overpowering impression made upon all who considered him and wrote of him, could not be ignored or in any essential altered. Neither Mark nor Matthew had an idea that Christ's power lay in the absence of power, whether miraculously or victoriously exercised, and yet each, with no thought of doing so, depicted one before whom instruments of power, Roman soldiers or hosts of destroying angels, shrank to insignificance, and the surrender of self became the greatest power of all.

3. The Gospel of Luke

THE GOSPEL OF LUKE was written by the man who wrote the Acts of the Apostles. The gospel is addressed to the "most excellent Theophilus," and written "that thou mightest know the certainty of those things, wherein thou has been instructed"; the Acts begins with a reference to "The former treatise I have made, O Theophilus, of all that Jesus began to do and teach." The tradition that the writer was Luke is as old as Irenaeus and it is backed by the fact that Luke was not a prominent person whose name would add weight to a book. There could have been no reason to ascribe these important writings to him except that he was known to be the author.

In the Acts he is Paul's companion on some of

101

his journeys, and occasionally Paul speaks of him
in the Epistles. He calls him "the beloved physi-
sian" and toward the end of his life he writes
from Rome, "Only Luke is with me." There was
clearly a warm friendship between the two and a
long association. And yet, just as with Mark,
Paul's theology made no impression on Luke.
There is nothing in his gospel any more than in
Mark's about Adam's sin and Christ being the
sacrifice offered to God to enable Him to forgive
sin. There is nothing of the kind in the Acts, even
in the speeches ascribed to Paul. It is certainly
possible that Paul had told Luke—and Mark, too
—that to write Christ's life on earth was of no importance and might even be harmful to Christians, leading them away from the contemplation
of the risen Christ to dwell upon him "in the
flesh," which Paul thought undesirable. This was
a conviction which had guided him throughout
his life as a Christian, from the time when he
chose to go away by himself to think out the implications of the vision he had had of Christ instead of seeking the disciples to learn about Christ
and what he had come to teach men. Paul cared
little for all that. Mark and Luke believed it to be
of vital importance. This sharp difference may
have come to the fore while Paul was still alive,
and may have caused them to reject his entire
interpretation of Christ. Whatever the reason, it
is certain they rejected it. There is not a particle

102

of Pauline theology in Luke any more than in Mark.

Luke drew on several authorities just as Matthew did. He had his own private source or sources of information; he used Mark as well; and also another from whom he took the sayings which in Matthew make up the Sermon on the Mount. Luke followed this authority he shared with Matthew more closely than Matthew did. His gospel shows that Matthew put together sayings of Christ which had been spoken at different times. In Matthew the Sermon on the Mount has no central theme and there is no connection between the several parts. One subject is dropped and another unrelated to it is taken up. Three consecutive injunctions are: "First cast out the beam out of thine own eye"; "Give not that which is holy unto the dogs, neither cast ye your pearls before swine"; "Ask and it shall be given you." Again, "Let your light so shine before men" is followed by "Think not that I am come to destroy the law." The Sermon does not read like one talk given at one time, but like a collection of sayings called forth by different events. That is the way Luke gives it. He reports almost all of it, but broken up and delivered to fit this occasion and that.

The Lord's prayer in Matthew is part of the Sermon, but in Luke, "As he was praying in a certain place, when he ceased, one of his disciples said unto him, Lord, teach us to pray. And he said unto them, When ye pray, say, Our Father which art in heaven." Then there follows a little parable about the importunate friend who will not take no for an answer, and then "Ask and it shall be given you; seek and ye shall find"; a clear development of the thought. But in Matthew these last words have no connection with what precedes. Also in Matthew "Enter ye in at the strait gate . . . Few there be that find it" comes directly after the golden rule, but in Luke it is the answer to one who "said unto him, Lord, are there few that be saved?" When compared with Luke the artificiality of Matthew's arrangement is evident.

There is one odd little difference between the two in regard to the place where the Sermon was delivered and the audience who heard it. In Matthew, Christ seeing the multitudes withdraws from them to a mountain and speaks to his disciples alone. But Luke's one long quotation from the Sermon which begins as in Matthew with the Beatitudes, is spoken when Christ came down from the mountain where he had spent all the night in prayer, "and stood in the plain" with his disciples and "a great multitude of people out of all Judaea and Jerusalem, and from the coast of Tyre and Sidon, which came to hear him." The passage reads as though Luke said that Matthew was wrong. Far from withdrawing into solitude to teach only his disciples, Christ sought the multitudes. He left the mountain and went to where the crowds could gather around him and listen to him. The point has interest because it suggests that Luke may have known Matthew, which goes against the accepted view that neither ever saw the other's work.

The private sources Luke used were for the most part superior to those Matthew knew. His gospel is much more beautiful. The account of the birth of Christ is a story unsurpassed for beauty if not unequalled, far beyond Matthew's. The annunciation too is told only by Luke, and Mary's answer to Gabriel, "Behold the handmaid of the Lord; be it unto me according to thy word." So too Gabriel's words to Zacharias, "I am Gabriel, that stand in the presence of God"; Mary's, "My soul doth magnify the Lord"; Zacharias', "To give light to them that sit in darkness and in the shadow of death, to guide our feet into the way of peace"; Simeon's, "Lord, now lettest thou thy servant depart in peace"—all are lofty poetry and all are peculiar to this part of Luke. There is nothing of just that order in Matthew or in Mark. Luke found them in some writer known only to him.

The two first chapters in which these passages occur are unlike the rest of the gospel in the strong Jewish feeling they show as well as in their poetry, so reminiscent of the Old Testament. Phrases abound such as "Our father Abraham," "God's servant Israel," "The holy prophets," "The oath which he sware to Abraham." Above all, the very essence of the Messianic hope is in Gabriel's words to Mary, "He shall be great, and shall be called the Son of the Highest: and the Lord God shall give unto him the throne of his father David: and he shall reign over the house of Jacob forever," one sentence which contains all the ages-old expectation of the Jews. It is never alluded to again in the gospel. Luke does not present Christ as the Messiah anywhere else. The idea would have meaning only for a Jew, which Luke was not. Also he was writing to a Roman who would have despised a Jewish cult centred in the triumph of the house of Jacob.

The rest of the gospel is not Jewish, indeed it is occasionally anti-Jewish. Matthew would never have reported a word spoken by Christ favourable to the Samaritan heretics, but in Luke Christ commends them more than once. Also in Luke he arouses the furious anger of the synagogue by saying that Elijah's and Elisha's most notable miracles had been worked for Gentiles, not Jews. The first two chapters stand by themselves. Some devout Christian Jew wrote them. They may well have been added unaltered to the original gospel. The first verse of the third chapter would be a good beginning of a book addressed to a Roman: "Now in the fifteenth year of the reign of Tiberius Caesar, Pontius Pilate being governor of Judaea"—

Luke had another authority which he alone used. Some of Christ's most beautiful and characteristic teaching has come down through him, the parables of the Prodigal Son and the Good Samaritan, the Pharisee and the Publican who went up into the temple to pray, careful Martha and Mary who chose the better part. This unknown recorder of Christ was able to follow Christ's thought when it broke through all religious conventions. In Matthew the parable of the ninety and nine ends with the irreproachable statement, "It is not the will of your Father in heaven that one of these little ones should perish," but in Luke with the daring paradox, "I say unto you, that likewise joy shall be in heaven over one sinner that repenteth, more than over ninety and nine just persons, which need no repentance." Only Luke too records the equally strange words of Christ about "a woman in the city which was a sinner": "Her sins which are many are forgiven; for she loved much: but to whom little is forgiven, the same loveth little." These sayings bear the very impress of Christ, the challenge he flung down to the hard and fast categories of formal religious thought, but only Luke's special authority noted them.

He noted too teachings of Christ about the kingdom of God which were different from those in the two other evangelists: from Matthew, to whom it was largely a geographical and political entity, and yet somehow connected with the Day of Judgment shortly to appear; from Mark, who declared that Christ said, "There be some of them that stand here which shall not taste of death, till they have seen the kingdom of God come with power." Luke alone gives Christ's words to the Pharisees who demanded "when the kingdom of God should come": "The kingdom of God cometh not with observation: neither shall they say, Lo here! or Lo there! for behold, the kingdom of God is within you." God's kingdom is of the spirit only. Its coming will not be until men possessing it within shall bring it to pass in the world without. So Luke's authority declared Christ said, and yet in Luke when Christ speaks of it there is a note of urgency absent from Matthew and Mark. "And he said unto another, Follow me. But he said, Lord, suffer me first to go and bury my father. Jesus said unto him, Let the dead bury their dead: but go thou and preach the kingdom of God. And another also said, Lord, I will follow thee; but let me first go bid them farewell, which are at home at my house. And Jesus said to him, No man, having put his hand to the plough and looking back, is fit for the kingdom of God." Only one brief sentence in Matthew can match the impression these words give of immediate and overwhelming importance. In Luke alone Christ says the kingdom is not at hand: he "spake a parable, because he was nigh to Jerusalem [and the cross] and because they thought that the kingdom of God should immediately appear"; and only in Luke is God's kingdom a kingdom of the spirit. Nevertheless, far beyond Matthew and Mark with their conviction that it will be a swift and glorious triumph, Luke stresses the urgent need to work for its coming. It is men's first duty, beside which all other duties count for nothing.

The sternness of the words is matched by others Luke records: "And there went great multitudes with him: and he turned and said unto them, If any man come to me, and hate not his father, and mother, and wife, and children, and brethren, and sisters, yea, and his own life also, he cannot be my disciple . . . Whosoever he be of you that forsaketh not all that he hath, he cannot be my disciple." This passage is only in Luke, as also the words: "So likewise ye, when ye shall have done all those things which are commanded you, say We are unprofitable servants: we have done that which was our duty to do."

And yet there is also in Luke a tenderness and compassion beyond the others, as in the account of the sinful woman whose sins were forgiven her because she loved much, and in the parables of the Prodigal Son and the Good Samaritan. There is a special feeling too for Christ, a personal touch which reveals something, not much, but yet something of what went on within Christ. When he goes back to Nazareth after the temptation, Luke says that in the synagogue "he found the place [in Isaiah] where it was written, The Spirit of the Lord is upon me, because he hath anointed me to preach the gospel to the poor: he hath sent me to heal the brokenhearted, to preach deliverance to the captives, and recovering of sight to the blind,

109

to set at liberty them that are bruised . . . And he began to say unto them, This day is this scripture fulfilled in your ears." Outside of John this is the only specific statement Christ makes of the way he saw his mission when he came preaching the kingdom of God. He came to the pain of the world, to heal, to console, to set free.

Other personal touches too Luke gives. When Christ thanked God that he revealed the truth not to the wise and prudent, but to the childlike, "he rejoiced in spirit," the only place where he is said to have felt like that. Matthew and Mark speak of Christ's praying, but no more than the bare fact, while Luke says, "He went out unto a mountain to pray and continued all night in prayer to God." When Christ came within sight of Jerusalem "he wept over the city." Luke alone makes the statement so weighted with implications after Peter speaks his third denial, "And the Lord turned and looked upon Peter." Matthew also quoted Christ's poignant words to the man who offered to follow him, "The foxes have holes, and the birds of the air have nests; but the Son of man hath not where to lay his head"; but only Luke gives the even more poignant, "I have a baptism to be baptized with; and how am I straitened till it be accomplished." Luke is alone too (except for St. Paul) in recording the appeal to the disciples at the last supper, so touching because so natural— Do not forget me when I am gone— "This do in remembrance of me."

The last days of Christ's life, the Garden of Gethsemane, the trial, the crucifixion, are told by Mark with an incomparable simplicity and solemnity. Matthew, following him closely, yet adds details which far from detracting are truly an addition. His account sometimes surpasses Mark's. But it is otherwise with Luke. Mark was his authority as he was Matthew's, but he abbreviated him and he lost greatly thereby. In Gethsemane he tells of Christ's going away from his disciples to pray only once instead of three times as in the other two. Luke seems to hurry through the story as if he could not bear to dwell upon that record of pain. He pauses, however, to add an alleviation, an addition which weakens disastrously the austere record in Mark and Matthew of lonely anguish unrelieved: "There appeared an angel unto him from heaven, strengthening him." The interposition of this divine visitant gives an air of unreality to what in the other two carries a conviction of absolute, unsoftened truth as much as any other words in the gospels. Luke, it would seem, or his unknown authority, could not endure the thought that Christ must suffer alone and that God would have it that way. Yet, strangely, he adds another detail quite inconsistent with this explanation and quite foreign to his temper of mind: "His sweat was as it were great drops of blood falling down to the ground." Why he put this into Mark's account is inexplicable. Everywhere else he turns away from what is distressing.

At Christ's trial he omits the scourging and the mockery of the purple robe and the crown of thorns, all of which are given by John as well as by Mark and Matthew.

His account of the crucifixion follows the same lines. He would not set down the words Christ spoke in Mark's record when the final darkness came upon him: "My God, my God, why hast thou forsaken me." In Luke there is no blackness of desolation. All that Christ says is consoling and tranquilizing. The sun is darkened, it is true, but not the spirit. The cross seems set in some pure radiancy of light.

As the soldiers crucified him Christ said, from what depths of unshakeable and unfathomable assurance, "Father, forgive them, for they know not what they do," ten words only which contain faith in its totality, in God, in man: God is our father; men are cruel only when they do not know. If that saying were all that was recorded of Christ it would never have been forgotten. After that he spoke to the thief, strong words of triumph, "This day shalt thou be with me in Paradise," making the present agony so brief and the portal to such bliss that the scene became one of joy, not anguish. Last of all, "when he had cried with a loud voice"—what, we are not told—the serene "Father, into thy hands I commend my spirit" brought to the spot where three crosses stood with their burdens the peace of God which passeth understanding.

112

4. The Gospel of John

THE EARLIEST AUTHORITY for the gospels we know of is Peter. Mark goes back to him, and Matthew and Luke go back to Mark, as does John too, although far less. Peter is very important for the gospels. In all four of them he is the same person, clearly drawn and easy to understand. He was a leader among the twelve, an impulsive man, very sure of himself and always ready to talk. On the Mount of the Transfiguration, when James and John, the only other disciples present, were struck dumb with terror—"For they were sore afraid"— Peter's fright drove him the other way; he began to babble about building tabernacles, "For he wist not what to say," Mark comments. But he had to say something. When Christ spoke dismaying words about riches and the disciples faced a bleak prospect, it was Peter who stated baldly what was in their minds: "Behold, we have forsaken all, and followed thee: what shall we have therefore?" He was better than his words. He had not left all and followed Christ to get rich. He spoke like that only because of his firm conviction that he had more common sense than Christ, and that he had to call him back when he wandered too far away from what was reasonable. Once this complacency drew down on him the most severe words Christ ever spoke. He had asked his disci-

113

ples, "Whom say ye that I am?" and Peter had answered, "Thou art the Christ." But when Christ went on to tell them how far his life and death would be from that of the triumphant Messiah implied in the answer, Peter, breaking in with his sureness that he knew best, "began to rebuke him saying, Be it far from thee, Lord: this shall not be unto thee." Christ said to him, "Get thee behind me, Satan: thou art an offense unto me."

As Peter talked, so he acted, on the impulse of the moment buoyed up by his belief in himself. When Christ came walking on the sea, the other disciples "cried out for fear," but Peter was filled with delighted excitement. He called to Christ, "Bid me come to thee on the water," and when Christ said, "Come," he got out of the boat and started. But the wind was boisterous, Matthew says, and his assurance vanished. He began to sink and cried out: "Lord, save me. And immediately Jesus stretched forth his hand and caught him and said unto him, O thou of little faith, wherefore didst thou doubt?" There is an exact picture of Peter in the beautiful story. He failed in the end although Christ was waiting for him, but he did more than the others, who only sat in the boat and trembled. He had something they had not.

In spite of childishness and conceit he was capable of catching a glimpse of what Christ was and responding to it with all his heart. When the draught of fishes filled the boats, Peter "fell down at Jesus' knees, saying, Depart from me; for I am a sinful man, O Lord." Suddenly he saw Christ, and in that moment of illumination he saw himself and he prayed that touching prayer. Nothing approaching this realization is related of any of the other disciples.

Of course at the end he denied that he knew Christ. That is the fact chiefly connected with him, but to condemn him alone among the twelve is unjust. In his usual way, hurrying out eager self-confident words, he told Christ, "Though I should die with thee, yet will I not deny thee," only to do so three times. But when Christ was arrested Matthew says, "All the disciples forsook him and fled . . . But Peter followed him afar off unto the high priest's palace." Poor as the end was, he did more than the others. And when at his third denial, "the Lord turned and looked upon Peter," he went out and wept bitterly.

An unthinking, hot-headed man, completely sure of himself one moment and completely unsure the next, warm-hearted, of all the disciples most capable of an impulse of devotion, genuine even if short-lived, capable too of a vision of Christ clear enough to lift him to humility. Such was the disciple who was largely responsible for the first three gospels. Most of what Christ said passed him by. Others noted and recorded the sayings in the Sermon on the Mount. He had not given them much attention and did not remember them. Only a few of the parables had made any impression on him. But he had a true devotion to Christ, and in striking contrast to his inattentive ears he noted as no one else did the last days of Christ's life. Only he told what happened in Gethsemane and only he dared to record Christ's cry upon the cross, "My God, my God, why hast thou forsaken me."

His narrative was filled out by the unknown men from whom Matthew and Luke took their accounts of Christ's teaching, but Peter's impress remained. His simple and objective view of Christ was a major influence with Matthew and Luke.

But Christ had another reporter to whom simplicity was not natural, whose mind was not objective, who was as unlike Peter as two followers of Christ could be, the man who wrote the Gospel of John. Up to a comparatively short time ago he was held to be the apostle. In the last chapter of the gospel it is stated that "the disciple which testifieth of these things" is "the disciple whom Jesus loved," always believed to be John. But scholars today say that those words were added later and that the writer was not the apostle, but a disciple of his. It seems to make very little difference. Whoever he was, he had his own special knowledge of Christ, either at firsthand or through someone who had lived with Christ, listened to words he spoke unheeded by others, and meditated long upon them. Most fortunately for our knowledge of Christ the Gospel of John depends only a little upon Mark. This was a deliberate rejection on the author's part, for he knew Mark and occasionally made use of him. But, in contrast to Matthew and

Luke, he had views which could not be merged with Mark's.

There are many surface differences. John disagreed with Mark about the order of events and where they took place and how much time they covered. In deciding between the two, Papias' statement must be taken into account that Mark's authority, Peter, had paid no attention to what came first or last. As far as that testimony has weight John's order cannot be judged wrong merely because it differs from Mark's. But John's differences go much deeper than any question of time and place. John looks at Christ from a point of view quite unlike Mark's which deeply influenced Matthew and Luke, and his account of Christ's teaching has almost no resemblance to theirs.

His point of view was different because he faced a different world. His Gospel was the last to be written, not by many years in actual fact, but when a new and enthusiastic and uncompromising religion starts, matters can move quickly. A great deal happened in a short time. For a number of years after Christ's death, perhaps a full generation, the little band of Christians were united by a common experience and felt no need of a common creed. Christ dwelt in their hearts by faith and when they spoke of him to one another each understood what was meant without feeling any need of explanation or definition. They knew within themselves the power of the Holy Spirit; it never occurred to them to think whether he proceeded from the Father or from the Father and the Son. This was true even when the first three Gospels were written. There is very little material in them for the most determined theologian.

But by the time John was writing, things had changed. A new and a great danger was threatening the Christians. Not persecution. That had been with them from the beginning and it was no danger to the faith. It was strengthening and purifying. But strange beliefs were in the air, making their way into the minds of Christians, new ideas of Christ which put him farther and farther away from mankind. They were a denial that he had any share in humanity, that he had lived a man among men and suffered death. He could not have inhabited a human body, because all matter was inherently evil, created by an evil deity. Only the semblance of a man had moved upon the earth and hung upon the cross. Vague, grandiose fancies had begun to hide the figure of the Son of man living in a world of fact.

The community of Christians was growing fast; the world was pressing harder and harder upon them. They needed above everything else to keep the realization of what Christ had been and the sense of a close relation to him. Both were attacked by the new ideas. Christ was held up as infinitely removed from all things earthly, at an illimitable distance from human sorrows and trials and temptations.

This was the situation which confronted John. Christ's reality was at stake. He wrote his gospel to defend it.

The fact that he felt he must fight separates him from the other three. Nothing of that kind was in their mind. Peter, whose influence was pre-eminent with them, had never an idea of defending Christ's humanity or his divinity. He simply told what he knew; he did not reason about it at all. He recorded in plain words the agony in the garden and the blackness of utter darkness which fell upon the cross at the end without a thought of any difficulty because in Gethsemane Christ had not been sure of what God's will for him was, or because when he died he felt abandoned by God. Peter had not made any theory about Christ. He had lived with him. That was enough. Therefore he must tell others about him, ready himself to die for him.

But the author of John's gospel was a man of another order, spiritually and intellectually. His mind was not objective; he was not content with seeing the fact, he was bent upon the meaning. He had to think out and understand, and this necessity of his nature was sharpened by the times he lived in. Christ might disappear and a shadow take his place. That was what threatened Christianity. Others besides John saw the danger and rallied to avert it. Into Luke's gospel, which was the one specially favoured by the upholders of the new ideas, were inserted words supposed to have been spoken by Christ after his resurrection which definitely ascribed to him an actual body: "Handle me and see: for a spirit hath not flesh and bones as ye see me have. Have ye here any meat? And they gave him a piece of broiled fish and of an honeycomb. And he took and did eat before them."

To declare that Christ risen from the dead still depended upon food was one way of meeting the danger. It was not John's way. That was not the weapon he would use to fight for the faith in Christ's humanity. He would think the problem through, Christ truly human and truly divine, the revelation of God's meaning for men; also the bread of life, of which if a man eat he shall never hunger; the witness to the truth which makes each man free; the true light which lighteth everyone coming into the world. He wrote his gospel to show divinity entering into and abiding in humanity, and individual men able to overcome the world because Christ had lived and died in it and overcome it. As the Epistle to the Hebrews says, "Wherefore in all things it behoved him to be made like unto his brethren . . . For in that he himself hath suffered being tempted, he is able to succour them that are tempted."

Both sides were clear to John, and yet in spite of his great powers, perhaps because of them, he failed in a matter of pre-eminent importance. Bent though he was on establishing Christ's humanity, he left out of his gospel Mark's account of Gethsemane and Christ's last words on the cross. Both were far too important to be merely passed over. John left them out deliberately. His account of the crucifixion is his own, not like any of the others in any respect. Nothing is said about a convulsion of nature. The sun is not darkened nor the veil of the temple rent. There is no anguish of abandonment as in Matthew and Mark, no joyful serenity as in Luke. The story is told very quietly. Friends are near him who in the other gospels watch him afar off. Beside the cross stand his mother and "the disciple whom he loved," and he speaks to them, "Behold thy son," and "Behold thy mother," words so simple and natural they are hardly arresting as one reads. But they are the only words recorded of Christ directed in love and care to one individual. They lift a very little the veil that covers his personal life, his relation to his mother. "And from that hour that disciple took her unto his own home." Luke shows Christ's divinity upon the cross, John his humanity. So Christ says, "I thirst," and the human suffering is brought home as in none of the others. Last of all he says, "It is finished." There could be nothing less dramatic and yet the words are moving far beyond the peacefulness of Luke's "Father, into thy hands I commend my spirit." The struggle to open the kingdom of heaven to the suffering world was over. Christ could do no more. It was ended, and he accepted the end. No more than that, no rejoicing, no relief even, but acceptance. "It is finished."

It is an extraordinarily realistic account, sober and moderate and restrained as compared with the other three. Yet John would not admit to his gospel that Christ had prayed not to drink of the cup of defeat and death, and that he had felt deserted by God as he died.

It is impossible really to understand this refusal. It may be that such an idea of Christ was too human even for his own theory; his spiritual vision may have been blocked by the demands of his intellect. Or he may have thought that it went beyond what could be credited by his generation, so hard-pressed to hold on to any reality in Christ. It might endanger the very cause he was defending. Men fighting for a cause are not always the best judges of how to advance it. Fortunately Peter was not defending anything. He wanted only to tell the truth as he knew it, and because he did so the full record of Christ's humanity has come down to us.

But although John could not always rise to the height of his own vision of Christ, he was able to put into great words the faith he was contending for. He wrote: "In him was life and the life was the light of men. And the light shineth in darkness; and the darkness hath not put it out . . . That was the true light, which lighteth every man that cometh into the world . . . And the Word was made flesh, and dwelt among us . . . full of grace and truth." So he expressed for all men to come the doctrine which is the centre of Christianity, the Incarnation, God manifested in man. Years later, in his first epistle, he gave it an even greater expression: "Beloved, let us love one another: for love is of God; and everyone that loveth is born of God, and knoweth God. He that loveth not knoweth not God; for God is love . . . No man hath seen God at any time. If we love one another, God dwelleth in us . . . God is love; and he that dwelleth in love dwelleth in God, and God in him."

The peculiar elevation and solemnity of these two passages are characteristic of John beyond any other writer in the New Testament. To mark his singularity one need only compare the way he begins his gospel with the way the others begin. John's first words are strangely solemnizing: "In the beginning was the Word, and the Word was with God and the Word was God." Not so the other three: Matthew's, "The book of the generation of Jesus Christ, the son of David, the son of Abraham"; Mark's, "The beginning of the gospel of Jesus Christ, the Son of God"; Luke's, "There was in the days of Herod, the king of Judaea, a certain priest named Zacharias." These are all written in the same spirit. The writers are bent only upon introducing their subject clearly, untinged by awe; they are not moved by any sense of mystery. John stands alone.

He was alone too in his account of what Christ said. The first three evangelists had laid all their emphasis upon the part of Christ's teaching which had to do with men's bringing about the kingdom of God by doing the will of God. John's whole emphasis was laid upon what only Christ could do.

In the other gospels Christ's greatest discourse is the Sermon on the Mount. It is straight ethical teaching and completely objective. "If thou bring thy gift to the altar and there remember that thy brother hath ought against thee: leave there thy gift: . . . first be reconciled to thy brother . . . Whosoever looketh on a woman to lust after her hath committed adultery with her already in his heart . . . Resist not evil, but whosoever shall smite thee on thy right cheek, turn to him the other also . . . If thy right eye offend thee, pluck it out . . . Ye cannot serve God and Mammon . . . Whatsoever ye would that men should do to you, do ye even so to them."

In John, Christ's greatest discourse is in the three chapters which follow the washing of the disciples' feet directly after the last supper. It is not objective; it is personal, concerned only with Christ's relation to his disciples. "Let not your heart be troubled: ye believe in God, believe also in me . . . Peace I leave with you, my peace I give unto you. Not as the world giveth, give I unto you . . . Abide in me, and I in you. As the branch cannot bear fruit of itself, except it abide in the vine; no more can ye, except ye abide in me . . . I will see you again and your heart shall rejoice, and your joy no man taketh from you . . . In the world ye shall have tribulation, but be of good cheer; I have overcome the world."

There is a great difference in matter and tone between these words and the Sermon on the Mount. It is true that the two were spoken under widely different conditions. The Sermon is given by Matthew very early in Christ's life, and Luke agrees as regards the chief part of it. Moreover that time, directly after the temptation, is the natural and logical setting for it. When Christ began to preach, his subject was that men could bring the kingdom of God to pass by doing the will of God. He felt a great confidence in those early days. He knew with absolute certainty that if men would hear him he could teach them how to end the miseries they brought upon and suffered from each other. The way to the kingdom lay open to all who would do the will of God. In the Sermon Christ was telling in detail what God's will called upon men to do. But the discourse in John was spoken when Christ realized that the kingdom of God was not at hand. Defeat was already upon him and the cross was very near. He was leaving the little band who had followed him, and his last words were to tell them that the bond between himself and them would not be broken. Death could not touch it. These words would naturally be marked out from Christ's other talks with his disciples, but the truth is that so far as the personal tone is concerned, they are like all the rest of John's gospel; they are marked out as different only from the other three. There is one passage alone which strikes the note continuous in John, Matthew's "Come unto me, all ye that labour and are heavy laden, and I will give you rest. Take my yoke upon you, and learn of me; for I am meek and lowly of heart; and ye shall find rest unto your souls. For my yoke is easy and my burden is light." These words are strange in Matthew. They are of the very essence of Christ's teaching as reported by John.

He was a man greatly gifted. Such men hear, see, think, feel, what others do not. John heard Christ say what the rest of Christ's hearers paid no attention to. Certainly most of his teaching had passed over Peter's head or was forgotten by him. It is much more surprising that the sayings in the Sermon on the Mount made no lasting impression on him than that he dismissed it as visionary talk when Christ spoke about being the light of the world or the true vine. Ideas like that were not within Peter's scope. And on his side John completely disregarded what to the three other evangelists was the very substance of Christ's teaching. He left out the Sermon on the Mount, the parables too. In the battle he was fighting for Christ's reality and his close connection with his disciples, ethical teaching was not of instant importance. He mentions the kingdom of God only once. He could not give his mind to it when he who

came preaching it was being turned into a fantastic
unreality. John thought not of a community devoted to doing God's will, but of every man finding salvation from self in one who was the perfect
satisfaction of the longing desire of the heart, the
refuge and strength for sinful men, joy in tribulation, light in darkness, security in chaos.

"Whosoever shall do the will of my Father
which is in heaven, the same is my brother and
sister and mother." That is Christ's message in
the three first gospels. In John it is, "Abide in me
and I in you. As the branch cannot bear fruit of
itself, except it abide in the vine; no more can ye,
except ye abide in me." The two are different, but
they spring from the same root. The basic attitude
to life expressed by each is the same: self-suffi-
ciency ended, self-direction too. The surrender,
the abandonment, of self, to God's rule, the three
said; to Christ's way, John said, who was the Word
of God, expressing in himself God's meaning for
all men.

VI

Christ

In him was life; and the life was the light
of men. And the light shineth in darkness: and the darkness hath not put it out.
—John 1:4

WE KNOW FAR more about the life of Christ than we do about Socrates' life and a good deal more than we do about St. Paul's. Of Socrates, except for his trial and last days in prison, we have to make a picture out of stray bits of talk in Xenophon and Plato, and he was not given to talking about himself or encouraging other people to do so. We know much more about St. Paul. We know him in a way that we do not know Christ. He takes us into his confidence. That is not true of Christ in the Gospels. We are never taken into his confidence. He is given to us drawn with a wonderful clarity, no blurred outline anywhere, carrying an overwhelming conviction of reality, so that never could he have been imagined; no one would ever have wanted to imagine him. He challenged men's dearest beliefs and most cherished institutions.

He made demands that would have stripped the world bare of all it liked best. The person the Gospels show us is proved real by his difference from everyone else. But we know him only from the outside. The men who wrote about him did not understand him, although they loved him and believed in him and set down faithfully what he did and said no matter how hard and incomprehensible to them it was. But they could not tell what he thought and felt, for they did not know. We are on intimate terms with St. Paul; his epistles are also his confessions: the evil that he would not do and did; his weakness which was turned into strength; his passionate fervour, his depths of wretchedness and heights of joy; his love that could bear and believe and hope and endure. He differs from us only in degree, not in kind. But that is not true of the Gospels. They never lift the curtain to show what was taking place within Christ. We hear him, we even sometimes see him, through the wonderful power of the Gospel story, but there are no intimate revelations. The story is always told from an objective point of view. And yet by some indescribable magic Christ comes close to us, closer than St. Paul. "Peter sat down among them . . . And another confidently affirmed, saying, Of a truth this fellow also was with him . . . And Peter said, Man, I know not what thou sayest. And immediately, while he yet spake, the cock crew. And the Lord turned, and looked upon Peter." That is all St. Luke says. He makes no attempt to set before us what was in that look. But we do not need to be told. Something is released by that brief sentence. We are fired to lift ourselves up and strive to feel what Christ felt. That way lies discovery. It is as if a personal experience touched us of what went on within Christ when he looked at the man he loved who had just uttered the final betrayal, the man he understood, who had said exactly what he had told him he would say. The words send a ray of light upon that lonely figure, and for a flashing moment we see better than through all St. Paul's confessions of his joys and griefs and pains. Nothing can be set beside the Gospels for their power of illuminating by what they do not say. Their reticences are revelations. The evangelists stand apart from Christ. He is never explained, never even described; and yet we know him.

The record of his life has to do with only three years, perhaps less. Back of it lie thirty years, so far back that almost nothing in them can be seen. A twelve-year-old boy, talking to learned men in the temple at Jerusalem and asking his parents when they found him, why had they looked for him? Did they not know that he must be about his Father's business? but who, once they had taken him home, was "subject unto them." A lad who "increased in wisdom and stature and in favour with God and man." That is the sum total of our knowledge of his childhood. About his youth we know even less, only a single sentence in St. Mark which says that the people in his own town who resented his later importance said to each other, "Is not this the carpenter, the son of Mary, the brother of James and Joses, and are not his sisters here with us?" It would appear that he lived in his mother's house, working at his trade and doing nothing to attract the special notice of anybody. Even his brothers and sisters saw nothing wonderful in him. At any rate, they told no stories about him which seemed to his disciples worthy of record. And his mother we know was not given to talk. She thought about her eldest son, so St. Luke tells us twice—"Mary . . . pondered all these things in her heart," and again, "His mother kept all these sayings in her heart"—but if Luke knew anything of what she thought he did not tell it. At the end of these silent years there was a movement throughout Judaea, a revival movement. John the Baptist was preaching what St. Mark calls "the baptism of repentance for the remission of sins." Baptism, the symbol everywhere of the purification of the heart. "Wash you," said Isaiah, "put away the evil of your doings . . . Though your sins be as scarlet they shall be as white as snow." The people confessed their sins and John baptized them in the Jordan. With them Christ came.

It was a long journey on foot from Nazareth. The road must have been full of many others traveling the same way for the same reason, and he was never one to hold himself apart from people. He walked with them and listened to them as they told him what they had heard about John and the longing and the hope which was sending them to him. John's message was excellent morality, the sort of thing the prophets of old would have approved, and he gave it with a fiery passion and vividness of utterance that was very like them. Passion and practical good sense, that peculiar Hebrew combination. He told the people, wrought up to a high pitch of emotion, that it was all very well to be sorry for sin, but the real matter was to bring forth fruits worthy of repentance. What this meant was the simple and realistic practice of self-denial for the sake of others and fair dealing when one had the power to deal otherwise. He that had two coats should give away one, and he that had more food than he could eat should do likewise. To the soldiers he said, "Do no violence"; to the tax gatherers, "Exact no more than is your due."

This is what Christ heard as he waited on the bank of the river for his baptism. This was all John could give the people hurrying to him to be taught what to do to satisfy their hunger for something they did not know how to find, or even what it was. But John was great enough to realize his inadequacy to clarify and satisfy that dim groping desire. "One mightier than I cometh," he said, "the latchet of whose shoes I am not worthy to unloose: he shall baptize you with the Holy Spirit and with fire." Did those words reach Christ as spoken directly to him, a solemn and tremendous summons? It would seem that they did; that they came to him as a personal message, and he was not ready for it. Even after John baptized him and he saw the heavens open and heard a voice, "This is my beloved son"—even that exalting and fortifying vision was not enough to bring him to a decision. He did not yet see the way he should take. That must be true because directly afterward he went into the desert. "Immediately the spirit driveth him into the wilderness and he was there in the wilderness forty days, tempted of Satan."

It is so impossible to imagine what went on there, and it is impossible not to try. All alone for forty days, regardless of food, regardless of everything but the conflict within him. The three temptations recorded, clearly in a symbolic form, seem to have been temptations to use his extraordinary powers for himself. The first: "The tempter . . . said, Command that these stones be made bread." You are hungry. Get bread—not by working for it as others do. You are different. The second: "The devil . . . setteth him on a pinnacle of the temple, and saith unto him, If thou be the Son of God, cast thyself down: for it is written, He shall give his angels charge concerning thee: and in their hands they shall bear thee up." Prove how different you are. Convince the world by doing a wonderful, spectacular deed. Subtlest of all, the third: "The devil . . . sheweth him all the kingdoms of the world and the glory of them: and saith unto him, All these things will I give thee, if thou wilt fall down and worship me."

The most lofty end possible. What could he not do for the world when once he had gained power and position. The evil involved was a mere form, utterly insignificant in comparison. Christ said, "Get thee hence, Satan." Something like that the record seems to show. It shows too that he was aware of his powers and the tremendous possibilities they held. But whatever he faced and fought there, one thing is clear: when he came out of the wilderness all was settled. St. Luke says that when the temptation was ended the devil departed from him for a season. If he had other temptations to fight, there is not a word to indicate that he ever again questioned what he was to do.

He left the wilderness in the calm and confidence of a crucial choice made. He went back to Galilee and on the Sabbath in the Synagogue of Nazareth he read to the assembly a passage from Isaiah: "The spirit of the Lord . . . hath anointed me to preach the gospel to the poor; he hath sent me to heal the broken-hearted, to preach deliverance to the captives, and recovering of sight to the blind, to set at liberty them that are bruised . . . And he closed the book . . . And he began to say unto them, This day is this scripture fulfilled . . ." The words throw a light on the days in the wilderness. He had gone there not knowing what he would do with his life. He came away with the decision made, and with the decision he reached the full consciousness of what he could do. He could heal the broken-hearted; he could

137

open the blind eyes and set the captives free. He knew at last what his powers were and how he would use them. John's summons to him had finally been accepted. He would baptize men with the Holy Spirit and with fire.

The people of Nazareth could not take this from one they had seen grow up among them. They were "filled with wrath and rose up and thrust him out of the city," but from the rest of the country great multitudes followed him, and "Seeing the multitudes he went up into a mountain: and when he was set, his disciples came unto him: and he opened his mouth and taught them, saying,

Blessed are the poor in spirit: for theirs is the kingdom of heaven.

Blessed are they that mourn: for they shall be comforted.

Blessed are the meek: for they shall inherit the earth.

Blessed are they which do hunger and thirst after righteousness: for they shall be filled.

Blessed are the merciful: for they shall obtain mercy.

Blessed are the pure in heart: for they shall see God.

Blessed are the peacemakers: for they shall be called the children of God.

Blessed are they which are persecuted for righteousness sake: for theirs is the kingdom of heaven."

The Beatitudes are a series of assertions, un-supported, merely stated. Christ brought forward nothing to prove their truth; he pointed to no au-thorities; he used no argument. And those who heard him did not want any of those things, nor do we who read them. There is a realm of truth which stands by itself and is beyond argument. In an assertion there can be a finality which carries an instantaneous conviction that it is not open to question. No one has ever wanted to prove the Beatitudes. Through them Christ seems to give his answer to the temptations in the wilderness. The Sermon on the Mount is his first recorded speech. Whether it was so in fact or not, and whether it was delivered at different times, it would seem that the first part at least was spoken soon after the struggle in the desert. The Beati-tudes stand in striking contrast to the tempta-tions. In the wilderness thoughts of power had come to him, dazzling power, "the kingdoms of the world and the glory of them." In the Beati-tudes he rejects power. It has no part in the good things of life. It has nothing to do with happiness. The blessed—the Greek word means happy—are the humble, the merciful, the pure in heart, the peacemakers. Here at the very outset appears the immeasurable distance between his view of the purpose and the fulfillment of life and that of all others. He knew, he must have known, that it was so. He said in effect, I alone know what life can give. I alone know what happiness is.

He ended the great discourse on a note of solemn finality: "Therefore whosoever heareth these sayings of mine and doeth them, I will liken him unto a wise man, which built his house upon a rock: And the rain descended, and the floods came, and the winds blew, and beat upon that house; and it fell not: for it was founded upon a rock. And everyone that heareth these sayings of mine, and doeth them not, shall be likened unto a foolish man, which built his house upon the sand: and the rain descended, and the floods came, and the winds blew, and beat upon that house, and it fell: and great was the fall of it."

"And the people were astonished at his doctrine, for he taught them as one having authority." The supreme authority of an absolute conviction. He went counter to men's most cherished ideas; he was completely alone; there was not one to support him, not one who understood him; but he knew what he knew with perfect assurance. It was the truth, of which there could be no question, from which there could be no appeal. The prophets had been God's mouthpieces. They had prefaced their words with, Thus saith the Lord. Christ said, I say unto you.

This mastery was felt by all who confronted him. Some Sadducees, of the powerful priestly party, came to him—by that time he had a certain notoriety as an itinerant preacher—and they planned to put a question to him in such a way

that it would make him ridiculous in the eyes of
the crowd. They did not believe in immortality
and they told him a story about a woman who had
seven husbands and "In the resurrection . . .
whose wife shall she be? for the seven had her to
wife." From the experience of all their life they
thought they were invulnerable in their armour
of power and pride, and they were ready for their
laugh at the travel-worn wayfarer who faced them.
But, strangely, as they looked at him it was somehow conveyed to them that their scorn and ridi-
cule did not touch him, did not reach him. He
answered them very gravely. Laughter suddenly
became impossible. He told them their question
was one only ignorance could ask. They were
ignorant of the very matters which as priests they
professed to know. "Do ye not therefore err," he
said, "because ye know not the scriptures, neither
the power of God. For when they shall rise from
the dead they neither marry, nor are given in marriage . . . And as touching the dead, that they
rise: have ye not read in the book of Moses how in
the bush God spake unto him, saying, I am the
God of Abraham and of Isaac and of Jacob? He is
not the God of the dead, but the God of the living: ye therefore do greatly err." They answered
him nothing, not a word to oppose the stern rebuke. They were convicted of error before all the
crowd and they did not even try to regain their
ascendency. They had felt penetrating their pan-

oply of arrogance an authority so commanding that they were helpless to question it, and they went silently away.

A bystander, a scribe, of a class highly respected, who had listened to the astonishing interchange, stepped forward to try to test further this shabby stranger who convicted priests of error, and he asked him what was the first commandment. He was not rebuked. Christ answered that the first of all the commandments was to love God, with all the heart and the soul and the mind and the strength. And the second was like unto it: Thou shalt love thy neighbour as thyself. His hearer answered him, "Master, thou hast said the truth." These two commandments were worth more, he said, "than all whole burnt offerings and sacrifices." And Jesus said unto him, "Thou art not far from the kingdom of God." A single sentence that reversed the situation. The shabby stranger took command of it. It was he who tested the scribe, and the grave words of commendation were received as from one who had the right to pronounce a final judgment. "No man after that," St. Mark says, "dared ask him any question."

Once when he had spoken briefly against confusing food with religion—the rules about preparing meat were many and minute—and had said that nothing that went into the mouth could defile a man, but only what came out of the mouth proceeding from the heart, his disciples told him in dismay that the Pharisees, especially given to ritual, "were offended when they heard this saying." The disciples' anxiety was natural. The Pharisees were the bulwark of learning and religion, and Christ had offended these revered teachers. Did he smile as he answered, "Let them alone, blind leaders of the blind"? With careless power he dismissed them. They were the intellectuals of his world, with a great tradition behind them. They did not matter to him at all, for he taught "as one having authority."

The full awareness of what he was and what he had to give came to him as he was baptized and in his struggle in the wilderness, but during the long silent years in Nazareth he had much time for meditation. He must have turned the profundity of his thought upon life, upon the problem of life which is the mystery of pain, and it is evident that the time came when he reached the solution of it. He saw what could end the agony of the world. Life could be the conquest of pain. It could be the end of the evil men bring to men, going on and on forever, never changing. He saw the way out of this blackness. Nothing complicated, nothing hard to grasp. It was not bound up with explanations a man must first understand. It was a way of life, the way to fulness of life. "I am the way." "I am come that they might have life and have it more abundantly." It was the way of truth. "I am the truth." He was what he taught. "To this end was I born and for this cause came I into the world, that I should bear witness to the truth." "And ye shall know the truth and the truth shall set you free."

"He knew what was in man," St. John says. He understood human nature, the lower depths it could reach as well as the heights, but he set no limit to men's spiritual possibilities. They could become sons of God as he was the Son of God. Whoever did the will of God, he said, was his brother. Men becoming like him, a verse in Romans says, that he might be the eldest in a vast family of brothers. Thus the kingdom of heaven would be brought about. He saw human life as it could be, and in those first days it must have seemed incredible to him that he could not make the world see it. It is always incredible to everyone who has caught the least glimpse of what is true. Christ must have walked along the roads of Galilee, after he left Nazareth, with joy in his heart. He had within him the clear triumphant certainty of what God was, the Power behind all there is and also his Father, always with him, sustaining him. He saw the pitifulness of human beings who could yet rise to the glorious liberty of the children of God, and he knew the unique and tremendous powers within himself to lead them there.

"Follow me," he said to Peter and Andrew fishing by the sea, "and I will make you fishers of men." There is a great confidence in the words. "He went through every city and village," St. Luke says, "preaching the glad tidings of the kingdom of God." "I saw Satan falling like lightning from heaven," he said. "And he rejoiced in spirit and said, I thank thee, O Father, Lord of heaven and earth." "Can the friends of the bridegroom fast while the bridegroom is with them?" he asked. In the figure he used of his teaching, the foaming new wine too strong to be put into old wine skins, there is a sense of strong and exultant power. He sent the twelve out to proclaim, "The kingdom of heaven is at hand." "Fear not, little flock," he said, "for it is your Father's good pleasure to give you the kingdom." Then the change came. How should it not.

It was true that the way to life was open to everyone. Whoever sought it would find it. It was not barred by the necessity of first believing this or that. No creed had to unlock a door to it, no conviction of sin, no acceptance of a saviour. Any one who hungered and thirsted ever so feebly for righteousness perceived ever so dimly, had all that was necessary. "Ask, and it shall be given you; seek, and ye shall find; knock, and it shall be opened unto you." Nevertheless it was hard. The way was narrow and there were few who entered upon it. In what we have of his talks to the crowds which gathered around him there is an absence of all appeals to them to seek and find. He never urges them to follow him. On the contrary he warns them what the cost will be. He bids them count it first, as a man would who intended to build a tower, "Lest after he hath laid the foundation, and is not able to finish it, all that behold it begin to mock him . . . So likewise, whosoever he be of you that forsaketh not all that he hath, he cannot be my disciple." That was what they would choose if they decided to walk along the way with him. "Whosoever shall seek to save his life shall lose it; and whosoever shall lose his life shall preserve it." A requirement the most drastic there could be: Life lived no longer for self. A complete surrender to the service, to the will, of God.

This was the demand Christ made upon those whom the Gospels describe as great multitudes coming to hear him. He looked at them with infinite compassion, but he put nothing easy before them. They were poor and ignorant and suffering and as sheep without a shepherd, yet he abated nothing from what he exacted. "If thine eye offend thee, pluck it out." No intimation that perhaps a man could not pluck his eye out. He knew men could.

Even so, extraordinarily, he was confident, and the reason why was that the way he pointed them to was the one he had entered, and he knew, because he had tested it, that it led to the kingdom of heaven for which no cost could be too great and for which no cost less than all a man had would be enough. "The kingdom of heaven is like unto a treasure hid in a field, the which when a man hath found, he hideth and for joy thereof goeth and selleth all that he hath, and buyeth that field." It is "like unto a merchantman seeking goodly pearls: who when he had found one pearl of great price, went and sold all that he had, and bought it."

The glad tidings of the kingdom of God. That was a kingdom of service where service was the only reward, its own exceeding great reward. To Christ it was the simplest, most self-evident truth. Men could be happy in no other way. Yes—but it demanded a complete change in the basis of human life which from the beginning of things had been founded on everyone's getting all that he could for himself. Christ said, Live not to get, but to give. Only he who loses his life shall find it. Of course as he went on with this teaching men turned against him. He had nothing external to propose, no creed they could recite, no set of doctrines they could subscribe to, and feel safe. The immense body of theological pronunciamentos does not find any support in his sayings. Ritual and ceremonial observances which are so easy and reassuring met with no mercy at his hands. The Sabbath is made for man, he said, not man for the Sabbath. That is one of his great freeing sentences, breaking through men's muddled values, making human welfare the only standard. But what did his hearers think to whom the sanctity of the Sabbath far outweighed any mere human good?

Christ put before men no forms whatsoever and only one dogma, love, proved not by talking about it, but by living it. Of course they shrank back from that kind of teaching, and he began to see that they did. Again and again he asked, "Do ye not perceive?" "Are ye so without understanding?" "How is it that ye do not yet understand?" It was not lack of understanding; it was fear of what he was asking them. They felt that they were living decent lives, that they knew their duty as, for instance, their duty to their neighbour, the man next door, who could in turn be expected to do his duty by them, a fair debit and credit system. But Christ said anyone in trouble becomes thereby your neighbour. All who are suffering have an absolute claim upon you for help. A certain man fell among thieves who robbed him and left him wounded by the roadside. A priest came that way, saw him and passed on the other side. Very highly regarded men the priests were, not only the special servants of God, but under the Romans politically powerful. Then came a Levite, also a holy man and important. He did the same. But there came a certain Samaritan, a despised heretic who did not believe in the sanctity of the temple, to deny which was next to denying God himself. He had compassion on the helpless man, bound up his wounds, took him to an inn and cared for him. Which of these three thinkest thou was neighbour to him that fell among thieves? Dismaying words which widened the circle of duty to a circumference as great as the whole of the suffering world. And was a heretic to be set above the pillars of orthodoxy? Was only what a man did important?

Christ was even more explicit. He said at the

last judgment men would be judged solely on the basis of how they had treated others. Not one word about their belief, only how they had acted to the unfortunate. The King would say, "Come ye blessed of my Father, inherit the kingdom prepared for you from the foundation of the world: For I was an hungred and ye gave me meat: I was thirsty and ye gave me drink: I was a stranger, and ye took me in: naked, and ye clothed me: I was sick and ye visited me: I was in prison and ye came unto me." And when they asked—bewildered, for they had acted out of spontaneous pity—"Lord, when saw we thee an hungred and fed thee, . . . or sick or in prison and came to thee?" the King would say, "Inasmuch as ye have done it unto one of the least of these my brethren, ye have done it unto me." This was outrageous doctrine to men who had the fortifying consciousness of impeccably correct belief.

How many too in the listening crowd were shocked when Christ made little of family life. The Jews were a people with an intense family feeling. The narrow circle of the family, concentrated upon itself, was an invulnerable defense against the claims of outsiders. Christ broke it down. "Then one said unto him, Behold thy mother and thy brethren stand without, desiring to speak with thee. But he . . . said, Who is my mother and who are my brethren? And he stretched forth his hand toward his disciples and said, Behold my mother and my brethren. For whosoever shall do

149

the will of my Father which is in heaven, the same is my brother, and sister, and mother." A man's love for his own because they were his own was one thing. The love in the kingdom of God was quite another. It broke through all restrictions, family, nation, race.

Quite as bad, perhaps worse, was what he said about riches, about all private possessions. A young man came running to him, eager to learn about eternal life, a good young man who had kept all the commandments and yet wanted something more, with his longing need written on his face so that Jesus beholding him loved him. "One thing thou lackest," he said to the lad, just one thing. "Sell whatsoever thou hast and give to the poor." And the young man "went away grieved: for he had great possessions." And Jesus said unto his disciples, "How hardly shall they that have riches enter into the kingdom of God."

Whatever we hold about the Gospels as we have them, how much they have been worked over here and added to there, however that may be, there can be no possibility of doubt that all these words are Christ's. No one would ever have put them into his mouth, warranted to arouse bitter hostility, certain to antagonize the important, the prosperous, the rich. They are his own sayings. He did not want what we want.

When John and James came to him asking to sit on his right hand and his left "in thy glory," dazzling visions filling their young heads, Jesus said unto them, "Can ye drink of the cup that I drink of?" In the words there is something like a tender mockery of their childishness. They are not a genuine question; he knew the two could not know of what he was about to drink. They seem spoken as if he withdrew into himself to contemplate that cup which was then so very near. And he called the other disciples and said, "Ye know that they which are accounted to rule over the Gentiles exercise lordship over them, and their great ones exercise authority. But it shall not be so among you. . . . Whosoever of you will be the chiefest shall be servant of all." He valued not at all what we value.

Still more dismaying, the worst things he ever said, the most repelling and impossible, were what he declared he demanded of his followers when they were wronged and unjust claims were made on them. "Ye have heard that it hath been said, An eye for an eye, and a tooth for a tooth: but I say unto you, That ye resist not evil: but whosoever shall smite thee on thy right cheek, turn to him the other also. And if any man will sue thee at the law and take away thy coat, let him have thy cloke also. And whosoever shall compel thee to go a mile, go with him twain." This is more than a demand. It is an imperious command. It shows the fidelity of the writer of St. Matthew's Gospel that he recorded it, and also in a lesser degree St. Luke's who gives some of it. But no one else ever noticed it, not St. Mark, nor St. John. St. Paul never alluded to it nor St. Peter, nor is it ever mentioned in the Book of Acts. The words are so drastic, so extraordinary, that this silence is remarkable. But indeed there has always been a tacit agreement to forget them. Nevertheless this was Christ's way to end evil. He declared that the evil in the world could be ended on no easier terms. Wrong was never to be repaid by wrong or violence by violence. To fight oppressors, to conquer them and humble them—would that end oppression? He answered, No. Evil could be conquered only by good; hate be ended only by love.

Small wonder that as he went on he saw angry threatening people in the crowds around him. The common people still heard him gladly, but the others, the important men, the responsible pillars of society and the church, were outdone with his ideas. They would upset everything, patriotism, property, the church, the home. Perhaps they understood him better than his disciples did. Certainly his closest followers had no notion what he meant. James and John when a Samaritan village refused them a night's lodging, came eagerly asking in a happy excitement, "Wilt thou that we command fire to come down from heaven and consume them?" Poor Peter, struggling with ideas altogether beyond him, asked, "Lord, how oft shall my brother sin against me and I forgive him? Until seven times? Jesus saith unto him, I say not until seven times, but until seventy times seven." Bewildered men, all of them, who had lived with him in close companionship and had hardly made a beginning of perceiving what he wanted of them. "And he asked them, What was it that ye disputed among yourselves by the way? But they held their peace: for by the way they had disputed among themselves, who should be the greatest." That was a dispute they often had. At the last supper "there was a strife among them which should be accounted the greatest."

More and more he learned how alone he was. The crowds that came seeking him and listened to him, really wanted only marvels from him. "And he sighed deeply in his spirit and said, Why doth this generation seek after a sign? There shall no sign be given." "Yet learned he obedience by the things which he suffered," a verse in Hebrews says. "And being made perfect, he became the author of eternal salvation unto all them that obey him." There are a few indications of how he felt, his weariness and homesickness in "The foxes have holes and the birds of the air nests, but the Son of man hath not where to lay his head"; his question to the twelve when men were turning away from him, "Will ye also go away?" Most moving of all, as his certainty that he must die grew clearer, the longing to suffer it quickly and have it over: "I have a baptism to be baptized with, and how am I straitened till it be accomplished."

St. John tells, near the beginning of the Gospel, the story of the woman taken in adultery, but it reads as if it happened near the end. When she was brought before Christ he showed no sternness to the men who accused her; he uttered no denunciation of their detestable self-righteousness. He disregarded them. He stooped down and with his finger wrote on the ground, his thoughts seemingly far away from them. But they kept on with their angry "Moses said such should be stoned, but what sayest thou?" Not a man there who did not know enough of him to be sure he would not answer, Do what Moses said. It was a trap, to make him show himself against the law of God and so worthy of death. At last he lifted himself up and said, "He that is without sin among you, let him first cast a stone at her." And again he stooped down and wrote on the ground. He was far away from them. When he stood up, only the woman was there. He asked, "Hath no man condemned thee?" She said, "No man, Lord. And Jesus said to her, Neither do I condemn thee: go, and sin no more." Such quiet words, as of one very weary. No probing talk and appeal as to the woman of Samaria. It is as if he was by then in the valley of the shadow of death. He was withdrawing. He had done all that he could except die. But nothing is plainer than that as he went on toward death, despised and rejected of men, he spoke with greater and greater authority, great though it had always been: "Ye have heard that it hath been said by them of old, but I say unto you"— There is a clearer and a deeper note just before the end.

"The hour is come, that the Son of man should be glorified."

"A new commandment I give unto you, That ye love one another; as I have loved you, that ye also love one another. By this shall all men know that ye are my disciples. . . ."

"I will not leave you comfortless: I will come to you."

"Peace I leave with you, my peace I give unto you: not as the world giveth, give I unto you. Let not your heart be troubled, neither let it be afraid."

"I am the true vine, and my Father is the husbandman. Every branch in me that beareth not fruit he taketh away: and every branch that beareth fruit, he purgeth it, that it may bring forth more fruit."

"I will see you again, and your heart shall rejoice, and your joy no man taketh from you."

"In the world ye shall have tribulation: but be of good cheer; I have overcome the world."

"And this is life eternal, that they might know thee the only true God, and Jesus Christ, whom thou hast sent."

He came to Jerusalem for the feast of the Passover and he was welcomed enthusiastically as "the King that cometh in the name of the Lord" by crowds who had not the least idea of a kingdom where the greatest was the servant of all. He was a wonder-worker to them who was somehow going to free them from paying taxes to the Romans. The priests looked deeper. They were powerful and prosperous and they did not want any change. Certainly they did not want Jerusalem to be a place where the last would be first and the first last. They were shrewd and conscientious too. This talk of setting men free, free even from the Sabbath, was highly dangerous. Christ's declaration that he was the Son of God and that the divine life lived in him and also in others, that God dwelt in the hearts of men, was destructive of authority, of all law and order.

They determined to get rid of him. They did not think they would have much trouble. One fact was clear: he was a non-resistant and if he did not resist, the people would not rise. So they made their plans. Christ going to the temple soon after his arrival threw out the tables of the money-changers set up in the outer courts, and all the rest who were making their profit out of religion. St. Luke says, "He went into the temple, and began to cast out them that sold therein, and them that bought, saying unto them, It is written, my house is the house of prayer: but ye have made it a den of thieves." Some sudden passion of anger stirred in his heart as he came upon these cunning traders in religion. There was apparently no resistance. Even the priests did not interfere and the conscience of the city was with him. For a few days he went about freely and talked to the people. Then he was arrested in the Garden of Gethsemane where he was used to go at night. This particular night he knew the end was at hand. He said to his disciples, "My soul is exceeding sorrowful, even unto death: tarry ye here and watch with me." He was reaching out for their companionship, a hand to put his own into. Then he went a little farther and fell on his face and prayed, "O my Father, if it be possible, let this cup pass from me: nevertheless not as I will, but as thou wilt." "And being in an agony he prayed more earnestly: and his sweat was as it were great drops of blood falling down to the ground."

He went back to his disciples and found them all asleep. He said, "What, could ye not watch with me one hour?" Then his tender understanding of their childishness found their excuse. "The spirit indeed is willing," he said, to himself, not to them, "but the flesh is weak." He left them a second time and prayed, "O my Father, if this cup may not pass away from me, except I drink it, thy will be done." He was realizing now as he had not even when he first prayed, that the cup was not to pass away. Again when he came back they were asleep. "Their eyes were heavy," St. Matthew says. "And he left them, and went away again, and prayed the third time, saying the same words." When he came back the third time he did not need them any more. "He saith unto them, Sleep on now and take your rest." He had fought and won this battle alone as he had fought the first in the wilderness.

Gethsemane has been little dwelt upon except for the purpose of arousing emotion. Christ's suffering there has been set beside his suffering on the cross to display what our salvation cost him. Few have paused to reflect that many a martyr faced with tranquil and even joyous fortitude a death as hard. The real meaning of Christ's struggle is seldom considered. The fact that it was a struggle is disconcerting to many Christians who wish to think of Christ as humanly unreal, conscious always that he was not a man, but God, assured in every detail of precisely what would happen, removed from bewildered humanity, free from the anguish of uncertainty, with no need for faith because he had absolute knowledge. In Gethsemane he prayed, "If it be possible, let this cup pass from me." There he did not know; he was not sure what God's will for him was; he asked Him not to lead him into the darkness he saw before him. That cup he prayed not to drink of was not death nor death on a cross. It was the failure of all he had done, of all he had believed he could do. And he prayed, "Thy will be done"—which refuses to me what I know I can do for the suffering world; which chooses to destroy what I have begun to upbuild. Christ looked into the impenetrable blackness of the mystery of the Power which calls the stars into being and moves in the atom and through it he saw the light of God. He prayed, "Not my will but thine be done." That was his battle and his victory in Gethsemane.

158

With his arrest the crowds that had thronged around him melted away. His disciples all deserted him. Peter denied he had ever known him. No one was faithful to him, not even John whom he loved best. It was defeat, there could not be more complete defeat. There was not one in all the world to stand by him. The crowd—no doubt the same people who had cried to him a few days before, "Blessed is he who cometh in the name of the Lord"—were all shouting now, "Crucify him." No one ever was so alone. So they crucified him. "And he said, Father, forgive them, for they know not what they do." At that moment, as they nailed him to the cross and lifted it, his compassion for men was foremost, and his faith in them. The men who came to look at him said, "He saved others; himself he cannot save"—quite truly. His last hours on the cross were watched by his mother and a few friends. In St. Matthew's and St. Mark's record he spoke only once. Just before he died he cried, "My God, my God, why hast thou forsaken me."

Words which through all the centuries since have been a source of sorrowful wonder. No one ever denied that he said them. Never would anyone have wanted to make them up. They show as nothing else the fidelity of Christ's reporters. Terrible as they must have felt them, they wrote them down. Any effort to explain them is predestined to failure. Whoever understands them best shrinks most from enlarging upon them. One thing we know: if we set some radiant death, Stephen's perhaps, beside Christ's, we have a glimpse of something immeasurably greater and more profound in the agony of the cross than in the glory Stephen beheld as he died, and in some strange way Christ is closer to us. We read with awe those last words; they are beyond our grasp; and yet from the depths he reached he can touch all suffering mankind—because of the depths he reached. "Himself bore our infirmities." What would a serene death, a joyful death, a triumphant death, mean in comparison? In him the mystery of evil was shown at the moment of its greatest triumph: he died having failed, looking at the moment of death into blackness. And "behold, he liveth forever more."

VII

St. Paul

Are they Hebrews? so am I. Are they Israelites? so am I. Are they ministers of Christ? I am more; in labours more abundant, in stripes above measure, in prisons more frequent, in deaths oft.

Thrice was I beaten with rods, once was I stoned, thrice I suffered shipwreck, a night and a day I have been in the deep.

In journeyings often, in perils of waters, in perils of robbers, in perils by mine own countrymen, in perils by the heathen, in perils in the city, in perils in the wilderness, in perils in the sea, in perils among false brethren.

In weariness and painfulness, in watchings often, in hunger and thirst, in fastings often, in cold and nakedness.

Beside those things that are without, that which cometh upon me daily, the care of all the churches.

—II Corinthians 11:22–28

1. The Hebrew and the Greek

S T. PAUL was the first Christian writer. He began to write his epistles only twenty years or so after Christ's death, and he died some years before the earliest Gospel was written.

He had the same strange point of view which all the Christians show in the Acts. He worshipped Christ with pure adoration. He called him "the image of the invisible God." Christ's death and resurrection were the centre, the heart, of his faith, but he passed over what Christ had taught. He was deeply concerned to hold up right ethical conduct to his churches, but he never fortified them by referring to the great ethics of the Sermon on the Mount. To the Old Testament he often referred and when he was disturbed about the morality of

163

the Corinthians he warned them how terribly God had punished lust during the wanderings in the wilderness, but he did not say, "Remember the Lord Jesus, how he said if a man looked on a woman to lust after her, he committed adultery in his heart."

He bade the Romans feed a hungry enemy and if he thirst give him drink, and the words sound like an echo of Christ's, "Love your enemies, bless them that curse you, do good to them that hate you," but Paul claimed no support from that greatest authority. In the epistles he quotes Christ directly only once, the words spoken over the bread and wine at the last supper, and once indirectly: "I know and am persuaded by the Lord Jesus that there is nothing unclean of itself, but to him that esteemeth anything to be unclean, to him it is unclean."

He never refers again to anything Christ said, and the conclusion seems inescapable that Christ's teaching was of no importance to him. Others remembered it and handed it on to those who treasured it, and so we have the Gospels, but the evangelists got no help from Paul. And yet the whole object of his life was to teach men about Christ. But the vision he had seen occupied his mind to the exclusion of all that he heard of Christ from Christ's followers. He would not have Christ seen except in that glory of heavenly light. He turned away from memories of his life.

Quite as noteworthy, perhaps even more so, is

the fact that he never speaks of miracles done by Christ. His disregard of Christ's earthly life does not account for this because the miracles would have been the perfect prelude to his vision. He did not want to look at the dusty wayfarer who longed for a place to lay his head, who never spoke words of glowing appeal, who prayed in Gethsemane. Paul would not say one word to call attention to him. But the miracles, Christ walking on the water, commanding the winds and the waves, bringing the dead to life, showed Christ as it was the passion of Paul's life to have him seen. Yet he never alluded to one of them—and he is by a number of years the earliest Christian writer.

Christianity soon after Paul's death was given over to the cult of the miraculous. The proof of a saintly life was not so much what a man did when he was alive as the wonders he worked when he was dead, and they were wonderful wonders. Christians had the excitement of living in an atmosphere of magical doings. Paul has no responsibility whatever for this unfortunate development. He did not believe in Christ because of miracles. In this respect he towers high above the church.

One miracle there was, however, which Paul not only believed but wrote of continually, the resurrection from the dead, of Christ and of all men. But that is not to say that he believed Christ's bodily presence had entered the room where his disciples were gathered and demanded food to eat. That would be supernatural and the miracle Paul believed in was spiritual. The supernatural is only the natural raised to the nth degree. It is supernatural for a man to walk on the water, but the difference between that and walking on the land is a difference in degree only, not in kind. The spiritual is different in kind. Love, joy, peace, are spiritual. Christ eating fish and honey after his death would have conveyed to his disciples that immortal life is only natural life heightened to some unknown degree. Paul never said a word to support that idea. The Christ he had seen was not a physical body, flesh and blood. He was "a quickening spirit" and a victory over death was the victory of the spirit over sin. "Flesh and blood cannot inherit the kingdom of God," he wrote. "But ye are not in the flesh, but in the spirit, if so be that the spirit of God dwell in you." Christ said to the woman of Samaria, "God is a spirit."

The world in which Paul was born was divided by two major influences, Hebrew and Greek. In the Christian world which he was finally to enter, the Greek hardly existed; the Hebrew was all powerful. The first Christians were chiefly Jews and their holy book for many years continued to be the Old Testament, quite as much as it had been before they became Christian. In the Acts the speeches reported of the various apostles, which never quote Christ, constantly refer to

Moses and the prophets and the psalms, exactly as Paul does in the Epistles. Stephen's long defense of the Christian position, delivered just before he was stoned, is a review of Hebrew history from Abraham to Solomon, with one brief reference to Christ. Paul assures Agrippa that he has never said anything except what the prophets foretold. Peter tells the Roman centurion that all the prophets give witness to Christ.

In the hands of these first Christian teachers the Hebrew Scriptures were started on the course of being turned into a Christian document. It was natural enough. The Christian Jews had been brought up to revere a Book as their great authority, and they had as yet no Book of their own. They could not give up the support of the written word, God's own word. Here as so often Paul led the way which the church was to follow. He showed how the Hebrew Scriptures could be Christianized. They could be turned into an allegory. He wrote to the Galatians that Abraham's two sons, one Sarah's, a free woman, and the other Hagar's, a bondwoman, "are an allegory; for these are the two covenants; the one from Mount Sinai, which gendereth to bondage, which is Hagar. For this Hagar is Mount Sinai in Arabia and answereth to Jerusalem which is in bondage to her children. But Jerusalem which is above is free . . . Now we, brethren, as Isaac was, are the children of promise. So then we are not the children of the bondwoman, but of the free. Stand fast therefore in the liberty wherewith Christ hath made us free."

The church seized on this method of gaining the Old Testament for Christ. If Christian liberty could be proved by Abraham's repudiating Hagar and the son she had borne him, a wide field was open for proving almost anything. All Christians had to do was to declare that nothing in the Scriptures was really what it was said to be, but always something else. Allegory flourished unrestrained with Paul's sponsoring.

Paul called himself "a Hebrew of the Hebrews" and he had solid ground for the assertion. A foundation rock of his teaching was the two great basic Hebrew conceptions: "Hear, O Israel, the Lord our God, the Lord is one," and "What doth the Lord require of thee but to do justly and to love mercy." Everywhere a Hebrew went he carried with him two unshakeable convictions, the Lord God made heaven and earth and all that in them is, and He demanded one thing from men, to live according to the moral law. This belief was Paul's birthright as a Hebrew. The Holy of Holies was the law of right and wrong given men by Almighty God.

But Paul was Greek too. He was born in Tarsus, then a centre of the most popular Greek teaching of the day, the Stoic. The ideas it put forth were not those of the Greece of Socrates and Plato, and they proved finally more congenial to the Roman mind than to the Greek. Stoicism

168

took firm root in Rome and from there it spread through the Roman world. It showed itself to be truly a religion, with the conquering power all deep religious conviction has. In his youth Paul must often have heard Stoics discussing their belief. They would be among the people he met every day. It would be strange if he had never also listened to their great teachers in the town. Certainly he knew what they taught and approved it, at any rate in part. Zeno, the founder, had declared that there was one supreme God of boundless power and goodness, who was not to be worshipped in temples, unworthy to house Deity, but who dwelt in every man, uniting all into one great commonwealth where there was no distinction between rich or poor, man or woman, bond or free. In St. Paul's speech on the Areopagus he told the Athenians: "God . . . dwelleth not in temples made with hands. . . . He hath made of one blood all nations of men . . . that they should seek the Lord, if haply they might feel after him and find him, though he be not far from every one of us: For in him we live and move and have our being." The words are a statement of the Stoic creed.

The idea that God had made of one blood all nations was foreign to the Jew. Paul did not get it from his Hebrew teachers. Only a few sentences in the greatest of the prophets point to it. One of the most passionately held convictions of the Hebrews was that they alone were God's people, favoured and lifted above all others. When Paul turned decisively from it, consciously or unconsciously he was following the Stoics. So he was too when he declared that in God's sight "there is neither slave nor free," and when he wrote to a man on behalf of his runaway slave, "Receive him not now as a servant, but a brother beloved, especially to me." One of the greatest Stoic doctrines was their revolutionary teaching about slavery. Precisely at the time when Paul was in prison, a leading Stoic, Seneca, was writing, " 'They are slaves,' men say. Nay, they are men. Slaves? No, comrades." And Epictetus declared that "A slave is your brother who is sprung from God, of the same heavenly descent as you." Master and slave to the Stoic shared in the divine light that illumined all and so became each a brother to the other.

Most unfortunately for the church—and also for the slaves—Paul did not follow the Stoics all the way. He never condemned slavery. The Stoics were alone in repudiating it for many hundreds of years, except for an individual here and there. Ironically, Christians took Paul's sending the runaway slave back to his master as a welcome endorsement of the righteousness of slavery. That did him an injustice. His attitude was negative only. He did not ever trouble his head about human rights. They were not important at all in his eyes. Even a superficial understanding of him shows clearly that he would himself have become a slave with perfect cheerfulness if it had seemed to him God's will. How he would have conducted himself afterwards, how submissive and obedient he would have been to unjust and, perhaps even worse, to silly orders, does not have to be considered. But he would have died to maintain that a slave was the equal of a free man in the only ways that mattered to him. "Ye are all children of God. There is neither slave nor free." That is the very voice of Stoicism.

To what degree it influenced him in other ways is impossible to say. He was grounded in the Old Testament writings and in the majesty of the great prophets' view of God. Yet lofty words heard from new teachers when one is young are apt to impress, and the Stoics' consoling and strengthening consciousness of a divine presence and a divine purpose was peculiarly adapted to take hold of Paul. "When you have shut your door," Epictetus writes, "say not that you are alone. God is in your room." "Knowing there is a purpose behind all," says Seneca, "I do not obey God—I agree with him. I follow him with all my heart and soul, not because I must." And Marcus Aurelius in his soldier's tent in the wilderness on the Danube saw life as "offering to God who dwells within you a soldier at his post ready to depart from life when the trumpet sounds, serene as he who gives you your discharge." No words except his own are more like St. Paul than sayings of the greatest Stoics.

He was the foremost Christian of all there have been, but he can be understood only if a place is given to the Hebrew in him and the Greek.

2. His Life and Thought

THERE IS ONE brief but notable verse in the Acts which marks the entrance upon the stage of history of two characters who for ages afterward were to play very important roles. The first Christian martyr confronts the first persecutor. "And they stoned Stephen, and the witnesses (It was written in the law of Moses, The hands of the witnesses shall be first upon him to put him to death.) laid down their clothes at the feet of a young man named Saul." That is the earliest mention of St. Paul in the Bible—he was called Paul later, we are not told why. On this his first appearance he bears all the marks of a fanatic of the most repellent kind, one who could watch with no motion of pity a man being killed in a brutal and horrible way. He was young, too, yet already hardened into cruelty.

He is an ominous figure as he stands there watching while a living man is battered out of all resemblance to humanity. He is the first persecutor we know of in history to whom we can give a name. The accusers of Socrates brought about his death, but they do not belong in this class. The true persecutor's creed is that objectionable opinions must be stamped out by killing the people who hold them. That was Paul's creed. Socrates' accusers did not want to stamp out an opinion; they wanted to kill one objectionable individual. The ancient world, generally speaking, was very tolerant of opinion. There had been some attempts to stamp out the Jewish religion, but they were religious wars rather than persecutions, and they grew more and more secular as they went on. Stephen's death showed a new spirit stirring in the world, one of the worst that has ever moved mankind. The young man named Saul at whose feet the clothes were laid to keep them from being spattered with blood, was destined to have a long line of successors. It does not take much imagination to see back of him, waiting to follow after him, a great host of men, all those who in the name of the true religious faith or the true political faith, have killed and imprisoned and tortured hundreds and hundreds of thousands, very many of whom died rather than give up what they believed. Foremost in the vanguard of that dreadful army St. Paul once stood.

He was a terrible menace to the little band of Christians. Great endowments were his. He was a man extraordinarily gifted by nature, with an indomitable will, a surpassing capacity of endurance, a master intellect, a brilliant power for organization, and a genius for leadership. It is impossible not to believe him ambitious in those early days, aware of his great powers and determined to make his mark. There was scope for strong men in Judaea then. Paul had reason to be confident in his undertaking to extirpate the Christians. What could they put up as defence against an able and ruthless man who had all the forces of fanaticism behind him. They were a feeble folk, the Christians, incapable of common-sense calculation, with absolutely no idea of safety first in their heads. Even so, they were increasing at a rate that threatened to make them a public nuisance, not to say a menace. If Paul could put a stop to the whole movement he stood to gain substantial credit. He would have taken a big step forward. So, the Book of Acts says, "He made havoc of the church, entering into every house and haling men and women committed them to prison." More especially, he presided over Stephen's death. Then "breathing out threatenings and slaughter against the disciples of the Lord" he started to Damascus to attack the Christians there.

Only a short time had passed since he watched Stephen die, perhaps only a few days. Those present at that death had seen a strange and arresting sight, the face of the man who was to be stoned. Looking on him, the Acts says, they "saw his face as it had been the face of an angel." Angelic serenity, the peace that passeth all understanding, angelic radiance, the glory of the shining of the true light, that is what they saw as Stephen "looked up steadfastly into heaven," and that is what Paul saw. When the other men there, ordinary common clay, were awe-struck at that look on Stephen's face, what did Paul feel? We know that that cruel young persecutor had deep within him an intensity of feeling, a capacity for love, for the utmost tenderness of love, never surpassed by anyone since. We know that underneath his hard surface was a sensitiveness, a power of perception exquisite as could be. What would such a one as that feel watching Stephen? He must have started on the journey to Damascus with Stephen's face perpetually before him. In his mind too were other memories, of the men and women he had "haled to prison," their fearlessness and gentleness and tranquility, counting it all joy to suffer for the sake of Christ. He would never have been able to blind those keen eyes of his or steel his passionate heart so that he would not see and be moved by what he hated to see, their unshaken serenity and steadfast courage. Now to that was added Stephen's joy and peace in the extremity of physical pain. As Paul rode along there must have gone with him an agony of doubt and a threat of an approaching agony of remorse.

From Jerusalem to Damascus is about a hundred miles as the crow flies. On the winding road it was much more. It was a slow journey, like all journeys in those days—nothing to do, no activity to divert a man's mind, just monotonous plodding on and on. It is easy to picture that young figure, no longer eagerly alert and on fire with fierce determination, but all deflated, jogging dully along, seeing nothing except what he could not blot out from his mind. Stephen had called upon Christ as he died. The two, Stephen and his Lord, were inextricably connected in Paul's misery. So through the long slow hours he suffered. Then, as the journey neared its end, suddenly that happened which changed everything. Anguish of doubt and despairing remorse were lifted from him never to return. Stephen's Lord appeared to him, and in a moment he was changed from persecutor to persecuted, from a man of hate and hateful deeds to a man who was to put into words as no one else ever, the innermost spirit of love and was to show forth its power by beautiful, heroic deeds. He saw Christ and heard him speak, and instantly the terrible struggle within him was stilled. A glory of light shone upon him, beneath which he fell to the ground as if physically struck down. A voice sounded in his ears, "Saul, Saul, why persecutest thou me?" He cried out, "Who are thou, Lord?" and the voice said, "I am Jesus whom thou persecutest." Then—the words are very tender—"It is hard for thee to kick against the pricks." Hard—that voice, that presence, knew. It had been hard past bearing. He had been like an untamed horse fighting against the spurs of memory and conscience and horror at himself. Paul had never heard the words, "Inasmuch as ye have done it unto one of the least of these my

brethren, ye have done it unto me," but he knew
how it was that he had persecuted Christ himself.
In that moment of great awe, of strange quietude,
submissiveness came to him, never felt before.
He said humbly, "Lord, what wilt thou have me
to do?" That, in the last analysis, was Stephen's
victory and the victory of those other nameless
men and women in prison, the victory so often to
be repeated in after days of the wronged over the
wrong-doer, the only complete and final victory.

So St. Paul, the founder of the Christian
church, became a Christian. Never from that
moment, as far as we can tell, did he waver.
Conflict within himself, bitter conflict, he was
indeed often to know. Through his whole life he
fought himself. But he never felt again any
shadow of doubt. There is an overwhelming conviction of reality when the things unseen come so
close that they are truer past all comparison than
the things seen. It came to St. Paul with a power
so tremendous that it was never afterwards even
dimmed for him. He lived always with the invisible more real to him than the visible. He had seen
the glory of Christ and had heard his voice.

The rest of Paul's life was spent as Christ's servant, with a single aim, to spread the knowledge of
him, rejoicing through all difficulties and dangers
and sufferings, until at the end he had the joy of
dying for him.

Directly after his conversion he tells us he went
"not unto Jerusalem, to them which were apostles

before me, but I went into Arabia," some desert spot, no doubt, to be by himself. It is extraordinarily revealing of the kind of man he was that at the beginning of this completely new life he did not want help from others. He felt no need for support, for reassurance, no desire to talk to those who had seen Christ and lived with him. And yet he knew almost nothing of him who had now become his Lord and Master. But he wished to know nothing except the vision he had seen. That was sufficient for him and throughout his life it remained sufficient. At this crisis when his old life fell away from him, it was all the support he wanted. Made as he was, no man could teach him what he had to learn. He must be alone; he must make the tremendous adjustment from hate to love alone with God.

It was three years later that he went to Jerusalem, and how he spent those years we do not know. We do know, however, the result. Paul returned to the world of men with a conviction which swept away what he had been brought up to believe most ardently, that God was a national God with a chosen people, and a God who was pleased by forms and ceremonies. This was a conception, indeed, which had been utterly reprobated by the greatest men of his race. The early prophets of Israel had scornfully denounced ritual and favouritism alike in the name of the Lord. "Vain oblations," said Isaiah, "incense and Sabbaths and feast days an abomination to God. I am

178

weary to bear them, saith the Lord." They had
seen not a God who had a chosen nation, but "all
nations gathered to the name of the Lord," and
God saying, "Blessed be Egypt, my people, and
Assyria, the work of my hands." But their grand
outlook had long been lost sight of, overgrown
with all manner of pettiness. Paul rediscovered
it with the help of alien teachers. Greeks showed
him the truth Isaiah had known. God had made
of one blood all nations of men. They were His
offspring, no one of more value in His eyes than
another. Customs, forms, ceremonies, meant
nothing to Him in whom we live and move and
have our being.

To reach this point of view was a tremendous
achievement for one brought up in the rigid and
meticulous system of the day, a Hebrew of the
Hebrews, as he calls himself. He tossed aside as
of no account the rite which had been supremely
important to him, the very truth of God. Circumcision, he declared, was of no importance: "Neither circumcision availeth anything nor uncir-
cumcision." "I withstood Peter to the face," he
wrote, because Peter had refused to eat with the
uncircumcised. Alone by himself in the desert, in
that time of testing, Paul had seen the matter
most vital for every human being to see, the rela-
tive value of the things men do. His eyes were
cleared to see the important and the trivial as in
the sight of God. He rose to the conception of a
God in whose presence was no place for triviali-

179

ties. It is true that he did not always keep to that great vision, but if one thinks what it meant for him with his religious background and his fanatical bent ever to achieve it, his lapses, not many after all, seem very human and very understandable. They are only little blots. The real quality of his mind was that which Aristotle calls greatness of soul: a largeness of mental and spiritual outlook marked him. He sweeps away grandly the sense of superiority, so dear to the human heart, and always the great disrupting force, the most deadly of all in dividing men from each other. Actual superiority is the most unifying force there is. It brings understanding which means feeling with others, and disinterestedness which means putting others first. But the consciousness of being set above others because one has blue blood or a white skin or the correct method of preparing food or the unique knowledge of the truth, is a barrier that cannot be crossed and a never ending cause of the cruelty and the anguish men divided from each other always bring about.

Paul would have none of it. "Ye are all children of God," he says. "There is neither Jew nor Greek, neither slave nor free, neither male nor female," —that was one place where he lapsed—"but all are one in Christ Jesus." The words are a declaration of equality, that strange notion which has never been realized on earth and yet can never be banished from men's minds. It was fundamental to Paul: no human being was of more value to

God than another. Man-made distinctions, as, for instance, between the slave and the freeborn, were mere inconsequential superficialities which the followers of Christ would disdain to notice. Paul's attitude in this fundamental matter is not always esteemed at its true value. Of course the church was not able to live up to it. What would she not have made of the world if she had. But with all her deference to power and wealth and rank some bit of it she kept and still keeps. To give it up, to admit that an emperor was more important than a slave, she would have had to give up St. Paul. It was he who drew up magnificently and adequately the Christian charter. All men were free and equal before God.

Less important and less grand, but yet with grandeur and profound meaning, is the way he considered the formalities of worship, the ceremonies and fastings and holy days and the like, which get so continually and so inextricably mixed up with religion. They did not matter; they were trifles to be waved aside. He dismissed them all, with a kindly tolerance, but with complete finality. Paul did not denounce them; they were not of enough consequence for that. They were well enough if people fancied them. The only thing wrong was to make them important. "One man esteemeth one day above another. He that regardeth the day, regardeth it unto the Lord, and he that regardeth not the day, to the Lord he regardeth it not. One man believeth that he may eat all

181

things. Another who is weak eateth herbs." Certainly, Paul thinks, it is better not to confuse food with religion, but it really does not matter. What does matter is a spirit of good will and a readiness to yield in these trifling personal preferences. Good will is not a trifle. "Meat commendeth us not to God, but if meat maketh my brother to be offended I will eat no flesh while the world standeth. We then that are strong ought to bear the infirmities of the weak."

That perfect tolerance, that clear vision of what is actually and eternally important, was reached by the man who had watched Stephen die and who was prepared to kill anyone whose ideas did not agree with his own.

The Christian church could not rise to that height. Nothing is more curious than what the church has chosen to emphasize in the New Testament and what to ignore. The scale of values St. Paul perceived, his estimation of what is essential and what can be set aside, was too much for the church. Any day she declared holy had to be held holy by all at their peril. If she proclaimed a fast it was to be kept under threat of very unpleasant penalties. But when, as did sometimes happen, St. Paul fell from the heights that were really the home of his spirit, when he descended to uttering trivialities, the church seized upon them and made them sacrosanct. So she did when he wrote about the importance of women's covering their hair when they prayed. In view of church history there is nothing surprising in the church's taking over what was obviously of no imaginable significance and making a sacred custom of it, but that Paul could say it, is significant. What was most characteristic of him was a sure grasp of the essential, but sometimes he lost it and always when he turned his mind on women.

His distrust and fear of them was at the bottom of his denunciation of marriage which the church, of course, as a mere matter of common sense, had to ignore. He declared it to be a poor, ignoble thing, a weak concession to human weakness which those that were strong rejected. Only the unmarried cared for the things of the Lord. The married were limited to the things of this world. Some experience in Paul's early life had coloured all his thought of women. "I suffer not a woman to teach," he said. "Let her learn in silence with all subjection." Yet he was a highly educated Hebrew, learned in the scriptures, and the Old Testament is the only literature in the world up to our own century which looks at women as human beings, no better and no worse than men. The Old Testament writers consider them just as impartially as they do men, free from prejudice and even from condescension. Paul knew that a woman had judged Israel; he knew that they had been prophets inspired of God. But some black and bitter experience lay behind him and he wanted to put them once and for all in the background and then be able to ignore them. Of course this was not possible. There were some women he honoured and cared for. He praised one and another occasionally, but he never retreated from the position that they must always be "under obedience." The matter is important not only because it fixed the attitude of the church and so of the Christian world, but because it is an indication of a division within him which cost him bitter struggles and sometimes betrayed him. So he could say with one part of himself, "Neither male nor female, but all one in Christ," and with the other part, that a woman must be in all subjection. Such contradictions were almost inevitable, only what was to be expected, in view of the man he had started out to be and the man he ended by being. Between the two no reconciliation was possible; it had to be a fight to the death, and in such a fight it is next to impossible to keep all the issues clear always.

In Arabia where he conferred not with flesh and blood, but fought his battle out alone, he had faced himself, a man indifferent to human pain even to the degree of cruelty, ambitious, arrogant, an egotist who counted his own ideas of supreme importance and the anguish and the death of others as nothing when weighed in the scale against them, blind to all true values as only the fanatic can be. So Paul had seen himself. And he had found that he could be saved from himself. What the struggle was who can say, but the scars of it were always there and he always feared they might reopen. Indeed, it is truer to say that though he was saved, ever thanking God who had given him the victory, the struggle still went on. It was years later when he uttered that cry of anguish, "O wretched man that I am, who shall deliver me from the body of this death." The answer was immediate, "I thank God, through Jesus Christ our Lord." Yet the struggle went on. "With the mind I serve the law of God, but with the flesh the law of sin." The body, always the body, "our vile body," he calls it. "I buffet my body and bring it under," he said sternly. Back of the words is a burning memory of past defeats and an acute sense of present danger. "The evil that I would not, that I do."

His life was a battle. He could never take it peacefully, not with all his untroubled faith in Christ, not with his deep knowledge of the peace of God which passeth all understanding. He had to tread another path. "I am crucified with Christ," he said, "nevertheless I live." "They that are Christ's have crucified the flesh." That was the only way he could conquer, kill himself, hang upon his cross and die to all that his ardent, passionate, powerful nature drove him toward. What he suffered we can only guess. That he never yielded we can believe. "We are more than conquerors through him that loved us," he said.

This battle that went on within him at the cost of agony, is not to be confused with the warfare against the forces of evil outside, the good fight of faith which he fought with an exultant spirit, wrestling gloriously not against flesh and blood, but against principalities, against powers, against the rulers of the darkness of this world. The kind of suffering that entailed did not cost him agony. It exalted him. He lists more than once his troubles and his dangers, the hardness he endured as a good soldier of Jesus Christ, "Labours more abundant, . . . perils of waters, perils of robbers, perils by mine own countrymen, . . . perils in the city, in the wilderness, in the sea, among false brethren, in weariness and painfulness, in watchings often, in hunger and thirst, in fastings often, in cold and nakedness. Beside those things that are without, that which cometh upon me daily, the care of all the churches." But hardships to the soldier were a matter of course; at worst they were only "our light affliction which is but for a moment, . . . while we look not at the things which are seen, but at the things which are not seen: for the things which are seen are temporal; but the things which are not seen are eternal." The man who spoke these words was invincible.

Paul would never have said, "The foxes have holes and the birds of the air nests, but the Son of man hath not where to lay his head." He did not care where he laid his head. There is not so much as a hint in his writings that he ever had to put down longing for shelter and comfort and safety. It is true he told the Corinthians, "We both hunger and thirst and are naked and have no certain dwelling place," but there is nothing of homesick longing in the passage; it is full of fire and resolution, a call to the church at Corinth to follow him in all extremities for Christ's sake. He never gave a thought to ease of life. His temptations were of another order. Hardship, difficulty, danger, drew him on. Once he writes that he will stay on in Ephesus because "a great door and effectual is opened to me—and there are many adversaries." He wrote that with the light of battle in his eyes. Fighting was born in him.

In the familiar twelfth chapter of Romans he bids Christians to be kindly affectioned one to another, "in honour preferring one another"— of course. Honourably to prefer another to himself was what Paul would always do. "Not slothful in business, fervent in spirit, serving the Lord" —each ringing phrase adds a line to his own portrait. "Bless them which persecute you," that too offered no special difficulty in his eyes, or to feed a hungry enemy and give him drink. But, "If it be possible, as much as lieth in you, live peaceably with all men." There he felt was a real task to take a man's full strength who must not be judged too harshly if he failed. Shortly before his death, looking back over his life, he said, "I have fought a good fight." Was he thinking chiefly of the fight within or the fight without. Either way the victory had been won. He had kept the faith, the cause which is betrayed every time men fall below their own possibilities.

On the whole the church has done him wrong. To be sure, she has preferred his teaching to Christ's, but that is because Paul was a simple man compared to his Lord, easily to be understood, whereas Christ was exceedingly difficult. "Good Master," the young man said to him. "Why callest thou me good?" Christ asked. "There is none good save God alone." Such words were very disconcerting to logically minded men who were trying to fit the Gospels into a clear, reasoned-out scheme. Not so Paul. They found him entirely comprehensible. It might be supposed that some of the things he said would present a difficulty as when he declared that God, "willing," he explained, "to show his wrath and make his power known," had created some men to be vessels of wrath fitted to destruction, and had predestined others to eternal glory, "for he will have mercy upon whom he will have mercy and whom he will he hardeneth," but these assertions did not trouble the theologians at all. Quite the contrary. They understood that kind of God. He fitted perfectly into their ideas and they adopted Him reverently and enthusiastically.

Paul never said anything that really disturbed them. So he was presented to the world as the master theologian. That was to wrong him. He did very little explaining why. His mind was pas-

sionately bent on how—how to overcome the evil
that confronts us, and no man that ever lived
knew better how than he. But it is true that he did
give some foundation to the stupendous structure the theologians raised, of which the chief
towers and ramparts were that all men were sinners from their birth and condemned as such because Adam had sinned in eating the forbidden
fruit. Therefore mankind, past, present and to
come, were under the wrathful judgment of God
whose absolute justice forbade the free forgiveness of sin. The only way His righteous anger
could be appeased was by the shedding of sacri-
ficial blood, by the sacrifice of an innocent victim.
Christ was crucified and the just God was satisfied. He required no more victims; a way of forgiveness was open for sinful men.

Paul cannot be absolved from a good deal of
responsibility for this. What he says is not in one
clear statement, only in stray sentences here and
there, but the gist of the matter is in them, the
conception of God held to unflinchingly by the
church for nearly two thousand years. In spite of
Paul's notable powers of mind and heart he could
not see what he had done to God. Neither did he
see the contradictions he was entangled in when
he set forth his charter that all men were equal
in God's sight, each one of absolute value in His
eyes, and then declared that He had created some
"to honour and mercy" and others "to dishonour
and destruction." It is difficult to understand how

this could escape him, but it did. In spite of his magnificent intellect the contest he was always carrying on within could not fail sometimes to disturb his ability to see. He was too great not to recognize his limitations. "We have this treasure in earthen vessels," he said.

What must always be remembered is that his aim, the passion of his life, was to set men free from the bondage of sin into the glorious liberty of the children of God. To explain God's plans and purposes was only of secondary importance.

St. Paul has been unjustly treated. Great men are judged by the heights they reach. Only a poet's best counts; his bad makes no difference at all. We never think of the poor lines Shakespeare could write, of the terrible verses Wordsworth perpetrated. None of that matters. People who achieve greatness anywhere in anything, are remembered for that. The rest of them is dropped out of sight. But St. Paul's worst has been given importance over his best. And yet the statements which demand for their validity a God who creates some men for eternal suffering and others for heavenly bliss are few and far between, while on page after page he has written words which are among the loftiest and most beautiful ever spoken. He, once the man of cruel arrogance, saw better than anyone else the greatness of humility and put it into great words: "In lowliness of mind let each esteem others better than themselves." "Let this mind be in you which was in Christ

Jesus, who being found in fashion as a man, humbled himself, and became obedient unto death, even the death of the cross." "Be ye kind, humble of mind, meek, long suffering; forbearing one another and forgiving one another." So he bade others do, and of himself he said, "Brethren, I count not myself to have apprehended; but this one thing I do, forgetting those things which are behind and reaching forth unto those things which are before, I press toward the mark for the prize of the high calling of God in Christ Jesus."

That was the spirit he showed, too, when toward the end of his life a runaway slave he dearly loved went back at his prompting to his master, a man known to Paul. No doubt the slave was in danger. Runaways were treated with extreme harshness. But Paul's letter to the master is a marvel of gentleness. It makes no demand; it claims nothing; it humbly asks a favour: "Though I might be much bold in Christ to enjoin thee, . . . yet for love's sake I rather beseech thee, being such an one as Paul the aged, and now also a prisoner of Jesus Christ. I beseech thee for my son Onesimus whom I have begotten in my bonds, . . . that thou shouldest receive him, not now as a servant, . . . but a brother beloved, specially to me. . . . Receive him as myself. If he hath wronged thee or oweth thee ought, put that on mine account. I Paul have written it with mine own hand, I will repay it."

Very close to this spirit was the great concep-

191

tion he reached after long conflict where the road to conquest lay. It was not for the strong, the resolute, the high-spirited. "When I am weak, then am I strong," God's strength made perfect in our weakness. Paul could not have had in mind Christ's hard saying, "Resist not evil." None of Christ's disciples ever noticed it except Matthew alone. Paul never even indirectly referred to it. Nevertheless these words of his are in some sort a commentary on Christ's. As if Paul were looking at Christ on the cross and seeing the victory won there by not resisting, through the surrender of self become the strongest power on earth.

It is Paul who named the Christian graces for us, not virtues which can be resolutely won, like truthfulness, but graces which are never won, but must come unconsciously, only through self-forgetfulness. "Love, joy, peace," runs his list, "long suffering, gentleness, goodness, faith, meekness, temperance." "Be ye kind one to another, tenderhearted, forgiving one another." These are the astonishing products of that fierce and fiery temper he once was.

The greatest and most beautiful words he ever wrote are about love, the thirteenth chapter of First Corinthians. It stands with the very best of the New Testament. But, strangely, it is not about the love of God, only about human love. And yet it was never in Paul's thought that we must reach the divine through the human. That idea was completely foreign to the Jew and Paul always remained, after his conversion as before it, a Hebrew of the Hebrews. He would never have said with St. John, "If we love one another God dwelleth in us." That was not the way he looked at things. He believed in Christ not because he had withdrawn into himself and found Christ speaking to him there, but because he was convinced that he had seen and heard Christ. What won him to Christ was that his eyes had beheld his glory and his ears had heard his voice. As for mankind, once he speaks of them as heirs of God and joint heirs with Christ, but everywhere else the extent of his belief in them is that they can be saved. Provided, that is, they are "called to be saints," "selected to be holy before the foundation of the world." Only so far his mind went, moulded to the model of the Old Testament.

But he was far greater even than the measure of his great mind. He had a power of feeling, which has hardly been surpassed. Love was a passion to him, an unsounded surging ocean. There he was at his greatest. With his whole being he felt the love of God: "For I am persuaded that neither death nor life nor angels nor principalities nor powers nor things present nor things to come nor height nor depth nor any other creature shall be able to separate us from the love of God." With an equal exalted intensity he spoke of the love of Christ which "passeth knowledge." "Who shall separate us from the love of Christ? Shall tribulation or distress or persecution or famine or nakedness or peril or sword? Nay, in all these things we are more than conquerors through Him that loved us."

But greater still than these great expressions of divine love is what he wrote of love here on earth. Here alone he could exalt the purely human. Sometime in his life he had loved greatly. He had known the love that transcends all selfishness and he had known the suffering such love brings. What he wrote is brief, only thirteen short verses, hardly a quarter of a page, and yet all of human love is there, its pre-eminence and the pain it is bound up with. Apart from it nothing men do is worth anything; "The tongues of men and of angels" are "as sounding brass or a tinkling cymbal." The mind, reason, knowledge, are profitless. "Though I understand all mysteries, and all knowledge, and have not love I am nothing." "Whether there be prophecies they shall fail. Whether there be tongues they shall cease, whether there be knowledge it shall vanish away," but love will endure. Without it faith, the very cornerstone of the church, is of no account: "Though I have all faith so that I could remove mountains and have not love, I am nothing." So too the very utmost of self-sacrifice: "Though I bestow all my goods to feed the poor, and though I give my body to be burned, and have not love, it profiteth me nothing." "Love suffereth long and is kind; Love thinketh no evil; seeketh not her own; beareth all things, believeth all things, hopeth all things, endureth all things. Love never faileth. And now abideth faith, hope, love, these three; but the greatest of these is love."

VIII

The Failure of the Church

The hour cometh when ye shall neither in this mountain nor yet at Jerusalem worship the Father.

. . . God is a spirit and they that worship him must worship him in spirit and in truth.

—John 4:21, 24

S T. MATTHEW says, "It is enough for the disciple that he be as his master." The simple matter-of-fact words are a reminder of the human reality of Christ. They are a summons back, away from complicated explanations of him and mysterious obscurations of him to the life he lived.

He called men to essay a tremendous venture. They could not rise to it, except a few here and there. And yet the picture in the Gospels of one who had lived and died with perfect selflessness could not be dropped from men's minds. Men would not pay the price he asked, but they could not forget him. And finally the compromise was arranged. Christ became chiefly a mysterious figure upon a cross, dying an awesome death infinitely removed from all other deaths. When he was thought of as having lived, it was a life equally

remote. He floated over the roads of Galilee, not a
human being, but a divine marvel. He had super-
human powers. He was not limited by time or
space. What was to happen lay clear before him.
He could calm the winds and the waves. There
could be no idea that men should be as he was.
Obviously they could not be. His life, removed
from all doubt and uncertainty, all temptation,
could have no real application to merely human
lives. All they could do was to wonder and adore.
So the church turned away from the Sermon on
the Mount and the Garden of Gethsemane to
an unfathomable mystery, God himself hanging
upon a cross. This was their way out.

The picture of the earliest Christianity given in
the Book of Acts shows a religion made up of two
things, a very simple conviction and a very clearly
marked way of life. The conviction is not expressed in various statements like a creed. It is
not formulated at all. Its centre, which was also
almost the whole of it, was that Christ had risen
from the dead. The glowing certainty that he who
died upon the cross had conquered death was the
all sufficient source of the strong joy and life of
the first Christians. Immortality was assured; the
crucified was the Prince of Life and alive forever-
more. The vivid sense of his presence awoke the
sense of personal sin and human helplessness, as
it had in Peter when he fell at Christ's feet and
prayed, "Depart from me, for I am a sinful man,
O Lord." But the knowledge of Christ brought

also the conviction of the forgiveness of sin. He who had commanded men to forgive until seventy times seven, would set no limit to his own forgiveness. This was the substance of the uncomplicated theology of the earliest church. An awed and joyful assurance of immortal life; repentance for sin and forgiveness; a consciousness of a change of mind to love the good and hate the evil, brought about by Christ's gift, the Spirit of Truth.

It was a belief easy to grasp. On the other hand, the Christian way of life was not easy to follow. There was no idea that men could take Christ as their master and be themselves comfortable and prosperous. The first Christians rejected the idea so completely that nothing a man had was his own. It belonged as he himself did to God. They shared their possessions with each other. "They had all things in common," the Acts says, "distributing to every man according as he had need." The result was, the author goes on to say, that "they gave witness with great power to the resurrection of the Lord Jesus." Men who so deal with the things that are seen are apt to be believed when they speak of things not seen. They were persecuted, too; they had full opportunity to prove that they had chosen to be Christians not to gain, but to give up. They were sent to prison and put to death and they rejoiced that they were counted worthy to suffer for Christ.

Christians thought of themselves as marked

out from others not so much by what they believed as by the way they lived. Their religion was
called the Way—Christ's way. They felt themselves committed to a manner of life which set
them apart. Christ's promise to them was, "In the
world ye shall have tribulation, but be of good
cheer: I have overcome the world." That was all
their expectation. They were here to bear witness
to the truth of Christ through the day-by-day sacrifices and the great crises of persecutions which
that entailed. Tribulation must be theirs because
they had chosen Christ. But he had overcome the
world. They had the triumphant conviction that
this life was only a brief prelude to the real life
which was unending. They were citizens of
heaven, exiled, indeed, for a period of hardship,
but, one that had its own peculiar joy of serving
and suffering for Christ. They had been lifted to
a level where selfish motives were not in control.
Within them they felt the power of the Holy
Spirit, Christ's spirit of truth, and their obligation
to spread the knowledge of the truth. From this
service they could keep back nothing they had or
were.

It was a condition of things which must have
lasted for a very short time. Perhaps it existed
only in the earliest days in Jerusalem. Paul, the
great shaper of Christianity, took no notice of it.
He urged his churches to give to the poor, but no
more than that. In later days he was troubled
about rich church members, if the epistles to Tim-

othy are his. Whether they are or not they show a great change in a few years from the Christianity in the Acts. There are men high in the church who are "given to filthy lucre"; Christians are seeking to be rich and falling "into a temptation and a snare, for the love of money is the root of all evil"; the way the women dress is shockingly extravagant; they trick themselves out with pearls and gold and embroideries. The days when all shared what they had with each other have been forgotten. St. James speaks even of "a Christian brother or sister" being "naked and destitute of daily food" and other Christians giving them nothing.

It is clear that even before the apostles died the demands made upon a follower of Christ had been notably lessened. Of course as the bars were lowered, more and more people came into the church. It was finally committed to quantity instead of quality. When it became the great state church, the religious authority of all Europe, hardly a trace was left of the idea that a Christian life was marked out as different from every other kind of life.

That was the time when the creeds began and the theologies developed. Men were provided for in every way. A member of the church—and that meant practically everyone—could live in the world as splendidly as his money allowed him. He could enjoy all manner of superiorities if he was rich and wellborn and be a good Christian if he repeated a form of words and, of course, attended the church ceremonies where they were repeated. An unusual person, either one with spiritual longings or one unable to face the demands life made upon him, had in the monasteries an honorable retreat in which the attainment of holiness was the avowed object. And between the one and the other the life Christ had lived dropped out of sight.

What, indeed, could be done with it as a practical proposition? Christianity would never be made to work efficiently by following Christ literally. He had had no methods people could adopt and put to definite use. He never laid down that matter of fundamental importance to an organization, clearly formulated conditions upon which one could enter it. He never demanded of the people who wished to follow him that they must first know this or that, the nature of the Trinity or the plan of salvation. He had not insisted on conviction of sin or consciousness of forgiveness or on any belief whatsoever. There was no basis in the Gospels for a theology people could come together on and have something forthright to hold to. The early church in Jerusalem which depended on Christ's holy spirit of truth in each individual and cared not at all for anything Christ had not cared for, was poor material with which to build something visibly strong and stable. So the great Church of Christ came into being by ignoring the life of Christ. The cloistered monks were as far removed from it as the magnificent prelates. The Fathers of the church were good men, often saintly men, sometimes men who cared enough for Christ to die for him, but they did not trust him. They could not trust the safety of his church to his way of doing things.

So they set out to make the church safe in their own way. Creeds and theologies protected it from individual vagaries; riches and power against outside attacks.

> Like a mighty army moves the Church of God.
> We are not divided, all one body we,
> One in hope and doctrine—

The church was safe. But one thing its ardent builders and defenders failed to see. Nothing that lives can be safe. Life means danger. The more the church was hedged about with Confessions of Faith and defended by the mighty of the earth, the feebler its life grew.

The life of the spirit could not be ensured by outside means, no institutions, however great and admirably run, had any power there; that way it could only be weakened. Here the artists, the poets, painters, musicians, were wiser than the men of religion. "To trust the soul's invincible surmise" was always their way. They took no thought for ensuring the safety of their art, but they were not afraid of music dying out of the world because it was left to individuals and never had money and never had influence. Good music, great music, needed no defence. It had a triumphantly strong life in itself which would continue among men forever. But Christians could not trust the life of the Holy Spirit like that.

Nevertheless, though it was imprisoned and stifled it never quite died. Even during the worst periods whether of cruel persecution or of arid disputations on "Fate, free will, foreknowledge absolute," the power of that little-regarded treasure, the way of Christ, worked in individual men and women who looked to the record of his life and tried to follow it.

I X

Faith

Now faith is the giving substance to things
hoped for, the proving of things not seen.
—Hebrews 11:1

THE POWER OF Christianity, the power of all religion, is sustained by that strange capacity in us we call faith, a word very commonly used and very commonly misunderstood.

Ages of faith and of unbelief are always said to mark the course of history. The latter part of the nineteenth century with the emergence of modern science is the usual example of an age of unbelief. For the perfect example of an age of faith people have always been told, and are being told today with especial insistence, they must look back to mediaeval days. Of course it is beyond question that during the middle ages religion was very powerful, indeed supremely powerful; but there is a question whether the kind of religion that flourished then was such as to stamp the times as an age of faith. Certainly, the underlying

motive which made many men profess religion
had nothing to do with faith. It was fear, which is
at the farthest remove from faith. There was a
horrible place called hell, as actual as the earth
itself, and once in it there was no escape to all
eternity. Safety from that horror could be gained
only by embracing religion. The idea was that of
a perfectly sure and most profitable investment.
Life was short, very short, indeed, during those
centuries; immortality whether in heaven or hell
very long; anyone could see the rationality of
foregoing present brief advantage for an endless
future profit. The appeal to the crystal-clear superiority of an eternity of bliss to a few years of
immediate pleasure is made by the most saintly
mediaeval writers; it is found in such masters of
the religious life as Thomas à Kempis and John
Tauler. It is evident that faith played no part
here; it was a mere matter of common sense.
Heaven and hell were substantial realities a man
could invest in while here below, and no elabo-
rate system of bookkeeping was needed to show
which should be crossed out. The so-called Ages
of Faith were only Ages of Certainty when men
were sure they knew and understood all things in
heaven as well as on the earth.

The church claimed to be the source of universal knowledge and her claim was allowed. She was
possessed of indisputable information on every
subject, not only heaven and hell and the roads
that led thither, but the way the world came into

being, how the heavenly bodies moved, what was the origin of man (and woman), why different languages arose, and so on, up to the exact constitution of the Holy Trinity. Nothing was as important as to accept these statements. Bliss or misery to all eternity depended upon doing so. How a man acted mattered not at all in comparison. The Inquisition burned people only for thinking incorrectly, not for living unethically.

During almost all the life of Christianity a wholesale subscription to whatever the church declared to be true was the one thing needful. Faith was something achieved or submitted to by the mind. To have faith in God was to accept what the authorities, men high in the church or learned in the book, asserted was the Truth. Often with a man of spirituality and intellect it came very near to being what the scoffers declared it was, believing what one knew was not so. Religion's chief function was to tell people what to think. It offered men that comforting possession, freedom from all personal responsibility. The mystery of human life was solved; no one need ever be disturbed by it. A neat dogmatic system was provided ready at hand, and to take this as the unalterable measure of the universe was faith.

It was a state of things which could last only as long as men chose not to question it. A day came when the men of free thought found that the universe was too big for the measure. That is the reason religion had a great setback in the nineteenth century. The church had tied herself up to explanations which were outmoded. When the light of science was turned upon them and they were shown to be false, she and the cause of religion stood discredited. As one after another of the ancient bulwarks, strengthened through centuries of theological thinking, gave way under the assaults of the scientists, the six-day creation, the Garden of Eden, the sun that stopped at the word of the man of God, the toppling down of the whole stupendous structure before astronomy and geology and physics seemed to undermine the foundation of religion. Complacent Christianity had a shattering blow. The theologians had claimed the entire outside universe and they lost it. They had not an inch left in it to stand upon. Ideas for hundreds of years proclaimed as final truth were mere childishness in the new universe that was opening.

The church had arrogated to herself what did not belong to her. She had insisted that the reason which finds proofs and causes was her own province, and that the field of the mind which observes and organizes facts was indistinguishable from the field of faith. Then the mind and the reason turned against her and she suffered a great defeat.

She went astray in a matter of supreme importance. She turned faith, without which there is no religion, into something which had no connection with faith. Early in her history her great

212

teachers began to urge it upon the masses as a matter of passive acceptance; upon people disposed to use their minds, as a matter of logical reasoning. The greatest of mediaeval teachers, St. Thomas Aquinas, said he had faith in Christ, first, because Christ had performed miracles, and, second, because he had been foretold by Old Testament prophets. Only third did he place the fact that Christianity taught men how to die. The argument as he saw it was clear: Only God can walk on the water. Christ did so. Therefore Christ is God. This to St. Thomas was the assurance of faith. This was the church's idea of faith when she had to confront modern science.

But when faith is supported by facts or by logic it ceases to be faith. When factual proof is possible or reasoning from an unquestionable cause to an inevitable effect, faith is excluded. Knowledge leaves no room for faith. When Christ said, "Blessed are they which have not seen, and yet have believed," he was describing faith. It belongs to that field of human activity which is concerned with making visible the things that are unseen. The field of faith has a common border with the field of art. That idea never dawned upon the great churchmen, but it would have been well for the church if it had.

During all the centuries of her life the church has made great use of art, but she has learned nothing from the artists. There was never an artist who did not know that he could not paint his picture or compose his music by thinking out the laws of beauty. If the church had seen the way to her truth as clearly as they did the way to theirs, there would have been no trouble and no defeat. Science never had any quarrel with artistic truth, and the artists never concerned themselves with what the scientists said was true. The painters and the poets and the musicians know that there is an order of reality in which intellectual assurance plays no part and the reason is unimportant. It is not measurable by the machinery of our minds, but it is real. "All great poetry," Keats says, "should produce the instantaneous conviction, this is true." The function of art, Tolstoi said, is to make that *understood* which in the form of an argument would be incomprehensible. There is a field where all wonderful perfections of microscope and telescope fail, all exquisite niceties of weight and measures, as well as that which is behind them, the keen and driving power of the mind. No facts however indubitably detected, no effort of reason however magnificently maintained, can prove that Bach's music is beautiful. Keats said of Shakespeare that he saw in him the power of "resting in uncertainty without any irritable reaching after fact and reason." What Shakespeare knew, he could not reason out and explain, and that troubled him not at all.

Definitions and analyses and all such contrivances of the classifying mind were never of any importance to the poets. Aesthetic dogmas might come and go. They never touched poetry. If a man of saintly life disagreed with the churchmen's rules, he suffered, in the so-called Ages of Faith, very painfully indeed. Not so in art. Aristotle's *Poetics* was long the critics' bible, but when Shakespeare was lined up against its rules and came out badly, it was not Shakespeare that suffered, but the rules.

This has always been the artists' way and therefore their truths are never left behind by the onward march of progress. Time does not touch their knowledge. Aeschylus is not superseded by Shakespeare; the centuries do not diminish Homer. But the truths of the mind are only for a time. They do not endure. They are perpetually cast aside and other truths take their place. Explanations, the very best of them, the highest reaches of the greatest intellects, have a brief life. "La clarté parfaite, n'est-elle pas le signe de la lassitude des idées?" The way of the mind is perpetually to doubt and question. Intellectual certainty is hampering. To be sure one understands closes the way to further understanding. But spiritual certainty never stands in the way of greater certainty. The perception of beauty does not hinder the discovery of more beauty. Love does not block the road to more love.

That final goal of human endeavour, knowledge of the truth, must be sought in many ways. In this world where the scientific truth is "an aggregation of protons and electrons," "a system of interrelated events," men produce from it an El Greco, the Oresteia, the Bach Passion music, an unselfish love, a heroic death. The part our reason can play in our search for truth is limited.

What the humblest artists knew, the keen minds that contrived the creeds and the catechisms failed to perceive. Perhaps it was not so much a failure in perceiving the truth as a choice which shut the truth out. The able organizers who took hold of the new young life of the Christian Church and bent their powers to defending it from attack and building it up into a mighty fortress superior to attack, demanded something more demonstrable than spiritual certainty, something more substantial than the vision of things not seen and manifested only in imperfect human lives. No solid foundation could be found there for their grand project, to establish in august majesty the great visible Church of God on earth. So they turned to the satisfying and by comparison almost solid ground of reasoned statements and logical deductions. That way one could arrive at something dependable. They produced creeds which were miracles of hairsplitting definitions of the eternal and infinite, and minutely reasoned out "schemes of salvation" which were clearly demonstrable from premise to conclusion. And very soon faith, which Christ had commanded, but never defined, which St. Paul had said was the power of religion without explaining why, became identified with the explanations and

definitions. To know them was to know the truth
and to accept them was to have faith.

This was to make an easy and shallow acquies-
cence of first importance. It was to elevate believing into a virtue, indeed into the one essential virtue, with the inevitable results of hypocrisy and
self-deception. It was to falsify the foundation
upon which Christianity rests.

Faith is not belief. Belief is passive. Faith is ac-
tive. It has a driving power. It is vision which passes
inevitably into action. "I have within me," said Eu-
ripides, "within my soul, a great temple of justice."
That is the only place where justice is. Outside
there is nothing but a dim distorted shadow of it.
But its unreality in the world does not affect its reality to us nor the passionate protest of our heart
when we see injustice. We know what justice is and
that it is of first importance. It is real though all the
facts say no. To know it thus as true, a truth one
will never give up, an idea one will never aban-
don, is to be halfway on the road to faith in justice. Only halfway; faith is more than conviction.
To have faith in justice is not only to perceive
what justice is, how great and how excellent, it is
also to be constrained to work for its realization,
to try to make justice come to pass. Although it
does not yet exist faith sees it, and acts to bring it
into existence.

There is one definition of faith in the New Testament, only one, in the Epistle to the Hebrews.
It has nothing to do with belief, but entirely with

action: "Now faith is the giving substance to
things hoped for, the proving of things not seen."
The way the author substantiates his hope and
gives proof of the reality of the unseen is not by a
series of statements which are to be accepted, but
by marshalling a long list of one life after another,
"a cloud of witnesses," who so lived that from
them men drew patience to run the race set before them. That is always faith's record, lives not
creeds. Christ never said, I will tell you the truth,
so clearly that you must understand, so convinc-
ingly that you must believe. He said, "I am the
truth." "His life was the light of men." Light
needs no proof. It needs only to be seen.

We are so made that we are able to perceive a
good which is utterly beyond us and when we see
it we must long to do something about it, to have
a share in it, if that could be. We needs must love
the highest when we see it, and love is always ac-
tive. Faith in Christ is awareness of his perfec-
tion, comprehending the utmost of selfless compassion and love, infinitely past our power to
reach, yet insistently driving us to reach it.

X

The Way of Christ

The people that walked in darkness
Have seen a great light.
They that dwell in the land of the shadow of death,
Upon them hath the light shined.

—Isaiah 9:2

IF THE GOSPELS had never been written, if we had only St. Paul's epistles, what we would know about Christ, far and away beyond everything else, would be "the exceeding greatness of his power," manifested in his death upon the cross by which "We were reconciled to God," in his glorious resurrection by which "Death is swallowed up in victory"; and in his continual presence, dwelling within men and giving them life and light, the life which "is hid with Christ in God," "the light of the knowledge of the glory of God in the face of Jesus Christ." This was the way Paul always beheld Christ, led thereto by his experience, first, of "the heavenly vision" he had seen, and then of the strength and peace and victory over self that the spirit of Christ within him gave him. If we had only St. Paul's writings we would know to the full all that faith in Christ can enable men to become. The testimony is so complete, so triumphantly assured, so magnificently expressed, that the great cloud of witnesses to Christ's power through the ages hardly adds to it except by weight of numbers.

But of Christ who walked the earth, who lived as a man among men, the origin of the heavenly vision, the source of light and the life abundantly at hand for the seeking, struggling soul—if we had Paul alone to tell us about him, we would know scarcely anything. The crucifixion and the resurrection he mentions over and over again, and gives a few details about the latter, but for the rest, all he says is that Christ "was made of the seed of David according to the flesh, and declared to be the Son of God by the resurrection"; that he was meek and gentle; that "on the night when he was betrayed" he divided among his disciples bread and wine, saying the bread was his body broken for them, the wine the new testament in his blood; that he "made himself of no reputation, and took upon him the form of a servant, and humbled himself, becoming obedient unto death, even the death of the cross." That is all. If we had only Paul we would know nothing beyond these few brief statements about Christ's life. It is a meagre account. No personality emerges from it. All Paul's vivifying enthusiasm inspired by his glowing adoring love of Christ, all his great powers as a writer, were devoted to putting before men not the Christ who had walked with men and taught them and healed them, who had prayed in Gethsemane and suffered on the cross, but the radiant Lord who had triumphed over death and was the glorious assurance of immortality to all who were victors through him.

To read Paul's epistles after reading the Gospels is to enter another world where there is vivid colour, rapturous adoration and transcendent experience and ecstatic joy. The atmosphere of the Gospels seems in comparison quiet and sober, very real. The profundity of Christ's feeling, the depth of his passion, had no kinship with raptures and ecstasies. Even the miracles hardly affect the impression of tranquility and moderation and mastery in Christ. The Sermon on the Mount, the parables, are marked by a grave restraint. St. Paul did not care to dwell upon that quiet figure. He turned away from it, and the church followed. Very few during the ages since have cared to

correct the portrait by the living face.

Therefore it is good for us sometimes to leave the company of the saints, apostles, martyrs, who all copied St. Paul's picture in their degree, and turn back to consider the strange Athenian almost five hundred years before Christ who saw many things in the same way Christ did, very important things.

Strangely enough, the very little we know about how he looked at prayer shows a resemblance to

Christ, and a great unlikeness to the saints in general. Of Christ's own prayers there is no record. What he said when he continued all night in prayer to God was never made known. We have only what he taught his disciples to pray. But the prayers of the saints were often recorded and they are for the most part so different from the Lord's Prayer that the comparison brings out the resemblance there is in the one prayer of Socrates which has come down to us. The saints when they prayed were given to exclamations and ejaculations, outcries of what one of them described as "a holy marvelling delight." There are many examples in St. Augustine: "O Thou Supreme, most secret and most present, most beautiful and strong! What shall I say, my God, my Life, my Holy Joy!" When one turns from such words to Christ, there is a sense of leaving a strange if beautiful land of awed ecstasy, and coming home. They said, "Lord, teach us to pray." And he said unto them, "When ye pray, say, Our Father which art in heaven, hallowed be thy name. Thy kingdom come. Thy will be done on earth as it is in heaven. Give us this day our daily bread. And forgive us our trespasses as we forgive those who trespass against us. And lead us not into temptation, but deliver us from evil. For thine is the kingdom and the power and the glory, forever and ever."

There is no transport of joyful emotion here. The prayer is tranquil, the tranquility of perfect assurance. A great simplicity and directness are in the words, and a realistic recognition of men's daily needs seen with an incomparable elevation and beauty. The saints prized the uncommon. Christ saw the dignity and worth of the things that are common to all.

Something like that is in Socrates' prayer: "Give me beauty in the inward soul; and may the inward and the outer man be at one. May I reckon wisdom to be wealth, and may I have so much gold as a temperate man and only he can bear and carry. . . . This prayer, I think, is enough for me." The quiet words which yet say so much, are closer to Christ than is St. Augustine.

Socrates' approach to life had a resemblance to Christ's. His temper of mind inclined to moderation and away from enthusiasms. When he talked it was never with the eloquence of soul-stirring appeal. He was bent upon one thing alone, the truth, and for that search calmness is needed and dispassionateness and, above all, freedom from self. Thoughts of rewards and punishments, heaven and hell, saving one's own soul, can only block the road. "And I would ask you to be thinking of the truth and not of Socrates." That wonderful speech in the prison clears our eyes from all the mass of selfish motives that have dishonoured Christendom, so "careful of safety, so careless of truth." Our vision is sharpened to see Christ. Socrates facing death with those words upon his lips is like only one other who said to Pilate: "For

225

this cause came I into the world, that I should bear witness to the truth."

Socrates sought the truth with a pure desire. He wanted only the knowledge of it, for himself and for all men. Through his search he was enabled to lift men to a new level where they saw truth not seen before, possibilities for mankind they had not dreamed of. He was able too to show them that the possibilities were actualities in his own life, and when they saw the highest in him they must of necessity love it. So much he could do and did. But one aspect of life, the strangest thing in it, did not engage his attention, the mystery of pain. He lived during a time of great distress in Athens, but he did not seek out those who laboured and were heavy laden, nor did they seek him. He did not see life in terms of suffering. Evil, indeed was present everywhere, men enduring wrong and, past all comparison worse, inflicting wrong. Even so, the good was what counted. That was his conviction and it carried him with unshaken fortitude through the bitter evil of his imprisonment and death. In this too he showed a likeness to Christ.

Christ spoke the Beatitudes; he did not set against them the arrogant, the unmerciful, the impure. He did not give the dark reverse of the picture because what he would have men see is that humility, purity, mercy, do not exist by virtue of their overcoming this or that evil. Mercy is not won by fighting cruelty and putting it down. It is as the light which shines in the darkness and which the blackest darkness is powerless to put out. When Christ said, "Resist not evil," he did not mean, Submit to evil (except to what touched oneself alone) but, Only goodness can end wickedness; only truth can conquer falsehood; only mercy and purity can put a stop to cruelty and lust. To him too the good was what counted.

But "he knew what was in man." His eyes saw all human life. He passed over no side of it and he turned the profundity of his thought upon the darkest problem of all, the problem of pain.

"Except a corn of wheat fall into the ground and die, it abideth alone: but if it die, it bringeth forth much fruit." These words are spoken by Christ in the Gospel of John. They express the innermost meaning of life as he saw it: enrichment through suffering and death. That is how he looked at the problem: good which could not be brought to pass otherwise, attained through pain.

Yet he never spoke a word to exalt suffering or to bid men seek it. That is the path the church soon took, but without any shadow of authority from him. He never sought or bade others seek what was hard because it was hard. He prayed in Gethsemane to escape the cross if it were possible. The self-inflicted pain the lives of saints are full of, is at the opposite pole from the way he looked at suffering and accepted his share of it. The starvation and the flagellation and all the devices for self-torture contrived after his death by passionate ecstatic men when the memory of what he had been on earth had faded and the Gospels had become the theologians' possession, show as clearly as anything in history the difference between Christ's way and the church's way.

Jeremiah said of the priests and prophets of his day, "They have healed the hurt of my people slightly." Christ knew the profundity of the hurt of the world and the way he showed it could be healed was as profound, his own way, not seeking to save his life, but losing it. This is my body which is broken for you. Perfect goodness, perfect selflessness, resulted in the cross, and through it men caught a glimpse of the meaning of unselfish pain. A man of sorrows and acquainted with grief—who else could speak to the world's agony? Anguish suffered for others—what else could prove love? Without the cross Christ could not have been seen. Light can be seen only in darkness. Therefore the most intolerable evil of all, the suffering and death of the innocent, was not meaningless and purposeless. They were the condition of the best and greatest good ever brought about. The cross pointed the way, not to any thought-out explanation, but to an apprehension of a purpose far beyond the goal of happy well-being.

That is how Christ looked at the great mystery of life. He did not state his solution in clear words for all to understand. That was never his way. He never spoke of suffering; he suffered. His life proved that there the deepest meaning of life lay. O my Father, if this cup may not pass away from me, except I drink it, thy will be done.

The Gospels are not an explanation or a theology. They are the record of a life. Men have asked of religion what religion does not give. You will ask it in vain for reasons and explanations, why this or that calamity has happened. Religion does not answer. It gives no reasons. It does not explain why. It shows men how. Our problem, the universal problem each one upon the earth must solve, is how to live. To that question the religion of Christ does give an answer, adequate for all needs and in all perplexities.

Christ saw truth in terms of life, on earth and in heaven. His statement of the truth was his own life; the proof was he himself. His criterion of knowledge of the truth was of the same order: "Ye shall know them by their fruits." He believed that few would find the Way he walked on, but there was no other way to the truth that makes men free: "Whosoever shall seek to save his life shall lose it; and whosoever shall lose his life shall preserve it"—the ultimate, joyful, never-to-be-lost freedom from self. "I am among you as he that serveth."

The kingdom of God is at hand. That is Christ's message. Everyone who seeks it can find it. No special preparation is needed, no special belief in this or that. Only to turn away from darkness to light, only to start in that direction. That is repentance, the one essential to entering upon the way. Then the light will shine more and more and the kingdom come nearer and nearer.

But the gate is strait and the way is narrow which leads unto life. It led Christ first to the cross. He said there would be few who would find it and follow it, but he set no limits to what they could do. Abiding in him they would bring forth much fruit. The works that he had done they would do also and even greater works. They could overcome the world as he had overcome it. The Spirit of truth would be with them forever and guide them into all truth.

Christ's way led to the cross, but it did not end there. No truth has been proved more conclusively through nearly two thousand years of history than that Christ lived on and still lives on today. He is the assurance that his way leads to life, in the kingdom of God which will never end.

The kingdom of God is at hand. There have always been people who lived in it. Times of fearful evil and misery come, but never a time when the kingdom is not at hand for those who seek it. It is here today, a power indestructible, unconquerable. He who proclaimed it taught "as one having authority." The record of his life has a strange authority. "The power of the good which lays upon us the obligation to fulfill it."